Does Every Child Matter?

Every Child Matters represents the most radical change to education and welfare provision in almost two decades. This book moves beyond a descriptive 'how to' framework to examine the underlying political and social aims of this policy agenda.

The authors' analysis reveals that *Every Child Matters* represents the Government's attempt to codify perceived risks in society and to formulate their responses. In doing so, children are made the strategic focus of much wider social policy reform, the effects of which are first felt in education. *Does Every Child Matter?* explores the ramifications of this along three key lines of analysis:

- The restructuring of the state beyond its welfare functions
- Changes in governance and the creation of new binaries
- A redefining of the education sector around the needs of the child.

This book provides a unique and insightful critique of *Every Child Matters* and its contribution to understandings of New Labour social policy. It locates the genesis of the policy in terms of its social, political and historical contexts and questions the validity of constructing social policy around issues of child welfare. Students, academics and researchers in education studies and education policy will find this book of major interest.

Catherine A. Simon is a Senior Lecturer in Education Studies at Bath Spa University.

Stephen Ward is Dean of the School of Education at Bath Spa University.

Does Every Child Matter?

Understanding New Labour's Social Reforms

Catherine A. Simon
and Stephen Ward

LONDON AND NEW YORK

First edition published 2010
by Routledge
2 Park Square, Milton Park, Abingdon, Oxon, OX14 4RN

Simultaneously published in the USA and Canada
by Routledge
270 Madison Avenue, New York, NY 10016

Routledge is an imprint of the Taylor & Francis Group, an informa business

Typeset in Sabon by
HWA Text and Data Management, London
Printed and bound in Great Britain by
TJ International Ltd, Padstow, Cornwall

British Library Cataloguing in Publication Data
A catalogue record for this book is available from the British Library

Library of Congress Cataloging-in-Publication Data
Simon, Catherine A.
Does every child matter? : understanding new labour's social reforms / Catherine A. Simon and Stephen Ward.
p. cm.
Includes bibliographical references and index.
1. Educational evaluation–Great Britain–Handbooks, manuals, etc.
2. Education–Standards–Great Britain–Handbooks, manuals, etc.
3. Education and state–Great Britain–Handbooks, manuals, etc.
I. Ward, Stephen, 1947– II. Title.
LB2822.75.S559 2010
379.41–dc22 2009050813

ISBN13: 978–0–415–49578–3 (hbk)
ISBN13: 978–0–415–49579–0 (pbk)
ISBN13: 978–0–203–84950–7 (ebk)

Contents

Abbreviations

ASBO	anti-social behaviour order
AYP	adequate yearly progress
BIS	(Department for) Business, Innovation and Skills
BME	black and minority ethnic (people)
CACE	Central Advisory Council for Education
CAF	Common Assessment Framework
CiC	children in care
CLDD	children with learning difficulties and disabilities
CPD	Continuing Professional Development
CWDC	Children's Workforce Development Council
CYPP	Children's and Young People's Plan
DCLG	Department for Communities and Local Government
DCSF	Department for Children, Schools and Families
DES	Department of Education and Science
DfEE	Department for Education and Employment
DfES	Department for Education and Skills
DHSS	Department of Health and Social Security
DIUS	Department for Innovation, Universities and Skills
DWP	Department of Work and Pensions
EAZ	Education Action Zone
EBS	education in its broader sense
ECM	Every Child Matters
EET	education employment and training
EHRC	Equality and Human Rights Commission
EiC	Excellence in Cities
EIP	education improvement partner
ENS	education in its narrower sense
EPPE	Effective Provision of Pre-school Education
ESEA	Elementary and Secondary Education Act (USA, 1965)
EU	European Union
EYFS	Early Years Foundation Stage

EYPS	Early Years Professional Status
FIMSS	First International Maths and Science Study
HAZ	Health Action Zone
HBAI	households below average income
HMI	Her Majesty's Inspectorate
HMSO	Her Majesty's Stationery Office
HMT	Her Majesty's Treasury
IMF	International Monetary Fund
IPE	inter-professional education
IPL	inter-professional learning
IQF	Integrated Qualifications Framework
ISI	Information Sharing Index
JRF	Joseph Rowntree Foundation
KS	Key Stage
LA	Local Authority
LAC	looked-after children
LEA	Local Education Authority
LMS	Local Management of Schools
NCLB	No Child Left Behind
NCC	National Curriculum Council
NCEE	National Commission on Excellence in Education
NDC	New Deal for Communities
NEET	(young people) not in employment, education or training
NESS	National Evaluation of Sure Start
NFER	National Foundation for Educational Research
NIS	National Incident Set
NPM	new public management
ODPM	Office of the Deputy Prime Minister
OECD	Organisation for Economic Cooperation and Development
Ofsted	Office for Standards in Schools
PCT	primary care trust
PEEP	Peers Early Education Programme
PGCE	postgraduate certificate in education
PSA	public service agreement
PSHE	personal, social and health education
PTA	parent–teacher Association
QAA	Quality Assurance Agency
QCA	Qualifications and Curriculum Authority
QTS	qualified teacher status

SCAA	Schools Curriculum and Assessment Authority
SCIE	Social Care Institute of Excellence
SEN	special educational needs
SEU	Social Exclusion Unit
SSLP	Sure Start Local Programmes
UNCRC	United Nations Convention of the Rights of the Child
UNICEF	United Nations Children's Fund

Introduction

Every Child Matters (*ECM*) is one of the biggest social policy initiatives of the post-war years, affecting all aspects of the lives of children and their families: education, social services and health. With its overarching notion of 'joined-up services', it includes a whole array policies and initiatives for health, social welfare and education. Its breadth and scope are bewildering. It involves almost every government department and every front-line professional across the public, private and voluntary sectors. *ECM* challenges long-held conceptions and assumptions about childhood, child-rearing, schooling and the way the whole welfare state is constructed. This book gets to grips with the range of policies by analysing the policy and the political beliefs underlying it. We show how *ECM* evolved and, in each chapter, look at its different features. We conclude with some speculation about the future of the policy from 2010. Throughout the book we offer the social, political and educational theory to inform the analysis.

Chapter 1 explores the political origins of *ECM* and the philosophical assumptions which underpin it. They derive from the 'Third Way' politics and the modernisation of the welfare state outlined by New Labour's first prime minister, Tony Blair. These theories have implications for the ways in which governments manage society and Chapter 2 looks at the ideas of 'new public management' (NPM) which were started by the Thatcher government in the 1980s and continued by Blair.

In exploring the origins of *ECM* we need to consider the international dimension to government policies. While *ECM* is unique to the UK and very much an invention of the British government, it is related to the *No Child Left Behind* programme which began in 1991 in the United States. In Chapter 3 we compare the two national initiatives and find that their similarities come from two shared worries: the global economy and the need for a skilled workforce, and public concerns about the treatment of children. Across the world, with the exception of Denmark, governments have spent more in the education of older pupils. For the first time in the UK there has been government recognition of, and a belief in, the importance of early-years education and care. This led to the development of *Sure Start*. Beginning in 1999 it should be seen as a pilot for the later and grander *ECM* plans to break the cycle of deprivation in society. In Chapter 4 we explain the thinking which underlies the *Sure Start* initiative as a modernist initiative to protect children and to invest in them for the future of the economy. *Sure Start* is based on the United States *Head Start* programme and the research from that, while showing the benefits, warns of some of the dangers. We examine some of the early research in the UK which has evaluated the value of *Sure Start*: whether it really works and is worth the money poured into it.

Childhood and the way we see children are socially constructed: what we expect of children is determined by social norms and political views. Chapter 5 examines the nature of childhood and how it is affected by government policy. We suggest that children's lives are determined by a risk-averse society and that the *Every Child Matters* agenda has tended to reinforce those limitations on child freedom and independence. The New Labour Government's social agenda for good behaviour, good parenting, and good communities was to produce educated citizens with the skills for a productive adulthood in the global economy. Chapter 6 looks at the economic policies which underlay *ECM* and we give a critique of the notion of economic wellbeing. In Chapter 7 we examine the position of children in care (CiC) and how government policy for the protection and safeguarding of children determined the *ECM* agenda.

Any social and educational policy assumes something about the nature of the child and the later adult which education and society produces. In Chapter 8 we explore the kind of citizen which is envisaged by the *ECM* outcomes and show how they relate to government policy on social inclusion, the regeneration of society and the creation of a 'new social order'. We look at the related issue of citizenship education in the National Curriculum for England and Wales and explore the idea of children as autonomous citizens with full civil rights.

ECM is not just about children: it is also targeted at parents, and in Chapter 9 we look at how parents are given a role in achieving the five *ECM* outcomes for children. The policy proposes a new relationship between parents and government, handing responsibility for the take-up of services to parents themselves. Parents are not a homogeneous group and there are stark differences between them. *ECM* recognises this and targets low socio-economic groups. It risks presenting a deficit model of working-class parents, imposing middle-class expectations and values on children and their families.

It was the Plowden Report (CACE, 1967) that first suggested multi-agency working: teachers should be in touch with social workers and health professionals. The 'joined-up' idea has to sound good, but in Chapter 10 we look at what multi-agency working really means and argue that there might be inherent problems. *ECM* ranges across all services for children, and of course that does include schools. While this isn't a book about schooling, in Chapter 11 we look at the effects of *ECM* on schools and the way they are changing to take account of the new requirements on them.

In writing about government policy it is always difficult to keep abreast of the rapid changes and events. The book was completed in December 2009, during the final months of the New Labour government which was first elected in 1997. *Every Child Matters* is the creature of New Labour and references to 'government' in the text are to the governments of 1997 to 2010. By the time the book appears it is possible, even likely, that there will be a different government. At the time, it was impossible to know whether a future Conservative government would sustain the funding for the *ECM* agenda in the current economic crisis. And it was difficult to know whether *ECM* would be consistent with Conservatives' philosophy of 'small state' politics. In Chapter 12 we offer some speculation about the future for *ECM*.

We have tried to make clear throughout that we are referring to New Labour policy of 1997–2010 and for that reason we often write in the past tense. But there may be occasions where the reader will need to note the date of writing and our not knowing what the future would bring. We can only apologise for inevitably being out of date!

Chapter 1

The political origins of *Every Child Matters*

Introduction

We begin with the political background to the *Every Child Matters* (*ECM*) agenda. The Victoria Climbié case and the subsequent Laming Report (HMSO, 2003) are often regarded as the reason for the Labour government's introduction of *ECM*. The case did receive a high level of publicity and focused the attention of policy-makers and the public. However, New Labour (1997–2007) had already decided on the development of social policy and had begun the process of reform towards *ECM* immediately following the 1997 General Election. The thrust of social policy reform was to break the generational cycle of deprivation into which children and families can become trapped. Tony Blair's 1996 declaration of three priorities, 'education, education and education', indicated the prominent position to be given to schools, and education generally, in promoting the new social democracy of what was called 'the Third Way' in politics.

> The Third Way ... draws vitality from uniting two great streams of left-of-centre thought – democratic socialism and liberalism – whose divorce this century did so much to weaken progressive politics across the West. Liberals assert the primacy of individual liberty in the market economy; social democrats promoted social justice with the state as its main agent. There is no necessary conflict between the two.
>
> (Blair, 1998: 1)

Background

Every Child Matters (DfES, 2004a) and *The Children Act* (DfES, 2004b) were the legislative spine of a complex social policy which cut across several government departments and ministries. This is evident in the five outcomes of the *ECM* agenda:

- being safe
- being healthy
- enjoying and achieving
- economic wellbeing, and
- making a positive contribution.

The Treasury, the Home Office, and ministries such as Justice, Work and Pensions, Transport, Health, Housing, Communities and Local Government, and Environment, Food and Rural Affairs all contribute to the *ECM* agenda; their work impacts significantly upon the five outcomes for children, young people and families. It would be naive to imagine that such an intricate reform agenda could be created in response to single tragedy. Rather, the Victoria Climbié enquiry, and the Laming Report (HMSO, 2003) with its 108 recommendations for improving child protection services, provided a popular rationale for the policy of social reform. This had been mapped out prior to the 1997 General Election and set in motion immediately thereafter (Rustin, 2004). Thomas and Hocking (2003) identify a host of 'targeted initiatives' introduced from 1997 'dedicated to reducing or eliminating negative impacts on children' (p. 59). These were:

- traditional 'education' reforms to raise educational standards with the introduction of the literacy and numeracy strategies;
- attempts to create a more child-friendly health service;
- public service agreements for looked after children; and
- a commitment to eradicating child poverty.

New Labour's first term of office 1997–2001 brought a range of initiatives:

- the National Child Care Strategy (1998)
- the creation of a National Family and Parenting Institute (1998)
- the Children's Fund (2000)
- the Children's and Young People's Unit (2000).

All point to the repositioning of the child and family at the heart of social and educational reform.

Understanding policy

Education, society and politics cannot be considered in isolation, and appreciation of the close interrelation of these concepts, together with economics and cultural values, are essential to the understanding of policy development over time. Traditionally there have been close ties between educational and social policy development within the UK, although there are acknowledged differences in emphasis according to region, especially since devolution in Scotland, Wales and Northern Ireland (Lingard and Ozga, 2007: 1). In this book we concentrate on central government and the English model of policy development and implementation.

There are several models or frameworks available which may be adopted as useful ways of understanding policy development and implementation. Taylor *et al.* (1997) suggest that policy analysis is about questioning what governments do: why and with what effects. Their three-point framework for policy analysis consists of:

- *Context* – the social, political and economic factors that have contributed to the formulation of the policy initiative: what were the problems or threats that government wished to address;
- *Text* – the content of the policy and how it is communicated. This is the domain of discourse analysis which seeks to understand the language and discourse types in a policy document to unearth the underlying political, social or economic assumptions;
- *Consequences* – how the policy is interpreted and implemented at all levels across departments and institutions down to practitioner level.

Taylor *et al.* also suggest a number of questions which help to focus the critical reading of policy and its implementation, including:

- How are the proposals organised? How do they affect resourcing and organisational structures?
- Why was this policy adopted?
- In whose interests? How have competing interests been negotiated?
- Why now? Why has the policy emerged at this time?
- What are the consequences? In particular, what are the consequences for both processes (professional practice) and outcomes?

Bell and Stevenson (2006: 12–13) add four further dimensions to this framework which help to identify and clarify the progression from policy formulation to policy in practice.

Policy formation

- *The socio-political environment*: Where does the policy come from? What are the overarching principles which drive it? Which are the dominant discourse types? First order values.
- *Strategic direction:* How is the policy shaped and defined? In what spheres will it operate, e.g. education, health, social services, youth justice?

Policy implementation

- *Organisational principles*: the parameters within which the policy is to operate, target setting, success criteria, patterns of control.
- *Operational practices*: organisational procedures, monitoring mechanisms, second order values.

Understandings of any given policy will vary. Those formulating a particular policy will have a different view of its content and values from those implementing or receiving it. Power relations and values underpin all policy. Who holds the balance of power and what are the value systems that dominate policy formulation and implementation are fundamental questions for those involved in policy analysis.

Understanding educational policy development in the UK

In reality policy development is not a neat and linear process; in the words of Bell and Stevenson (2006: 19) it is 'fuzzy, messy and complex ... the product of compromise, negotiation, dispute and struggle'. Furthermore, they argue that 'policy can ... be presented in part as the analysis of change and the way in which change is managed' (2006: 22). Change and the pace of change has dominated policy discourse in recent decades, particularly since the rise of Thatcher's New Right government in 1979, followed by New Labour and the 'modernisers' in 1997. What emerged through this 'change agenda' was the opening up of the state institutions of education, health and welfare to market forces and private investment. This was to alter the nature of these services and the manner in which they operated. Business models of standards, targets and accountability changed the relationship between those in government (both at national and local level) and those running or using the services.

What was known as the 'social settlement' (Clarke and Newman, 1997) based on understandings of the role of the 'family, nation and work' in the development of welfare policies and the construction of the post-war welfare state, was challenged and ultimately dismantled. The process began in earnest under the premiership of Margaret Thatcher (1979–1990) with her neo-liberal economic ideology. Most of twentieth-century politics had been dominated by the thinking of the economist J.M. Keynes (1883–1946): an equal society where, through taxation, the state provided for the weakest and most vulnerable, '[Thatcher's] plan was to reduce taxation, "roll back the state" and allow people to have greater personal control over their lives' (Ward, 2008: 11). Policies promoting home ownership, and the privatisation of previously nationalised industries and utilities such as the railways, gas, electricity and the water supply, created a new generation of share-holders with a stake in all manner of services and industries from banking to manufacturing. Such was the zeal for privatisation that Thatcher was later to be accused by Harold MacMillan, one-time Conservative Prime Minister, during his maiden speech to the House of Lords in 1986, of 'selling off the family silver'.

One consequence of neo-liberalism and the promotion of a 'free market' was the rise of 'individualism'. It was no coincidence that during the 1980s the young and upwardly mobile were able to take advantage of the redistribution of wealth from state coffers to private pockets. 'Thatcher's children' became synonymous with a preoccupation with competition, social capital, meritocracy and entrepreneurship alongside long working hours, high wages and consumerism, a trend which continued through the 1980s and 1990s. The self-centred, Randian perspective (Rand, 1964), and Thatcher's belief that 'there is no such thing as society' (*Woman's Own*, 1987) contributed to a widening of the disparity between the wealthy and the poor, with inevitable consequences for the most vulnerable in society, including children.

Every Child Matters: Context, text and consequences

As we have already seen, educational, social and economic policies are closely interrelated. When New Labour came to power in 1997 it continued the steady march of educational reform set in motion by 18 years of Conservative administration. Indeed, as Tomlinson (2005) points out, New Labour appeared to accept many of the underlying beliefs and assumptions of Tory policy-making during those years. Themes such as choice and competition, the rhetoric of 'raising standards' and the business model of leadership and management continued to shape New Labour policy from 1997. The driving force was a desire to remain competitive on the stage of the global economy. The rise of new technologies in the latter part of the twentieth century meant that Britain's strong manufacturing base was no longer a requirement for global economic supremacy, and many such industries were destined to close, or to move where the workforce was cheaper. The new growth area was to be in service industries. Rather than be dependent on largely unskilled labour, the new 'industrial revolution' of the late twentieth century demanded a highly skilled and educated workforce, one that could be more responsive to the changing world of work and the need for a wider range of transferable skills. The government saw investment in 'human capital' as essential. This concept is that 'human beings invest in themselves by means of education, training or other activities which raise their future income by increasing their lifetime earnings' (Woodhall, 1997: 219). In turn, this calls for a commitment to both 'knowledge and education' (Tomlinson, 2005: 90) with investment in lifelong learning and the 'subordination of education to the economy', all of which were evident in New Labour policy from the outset.

Indeed, as Tomlinson asserts, the link between education and the economy typified post-Second World War education policy. The adoption of human capital theory – the assumption that investment in skills and capabilities will enhance production – was to couple education and the economy more closely together.

> Human capital is the sum of education and skill that can be used to produce wealth. It helps to determine the earning capacity of individuals and their contribution to the economic performance of the state in which they work
>
> (Bell and Stevenson, 2006: 42).

The resurgence of human capital theory in the closing years of the twentieth century indicates government concern over its positioning on the global stage. It became the business of government to invest in human capital, even though the relationship between expenditure or investment in education and training and economic performance was questionable (OECD, 1996, cited in Bell and Stevenson, 2006: 50).

However, in order to facilitate the uptake of such education and training, attention has also turned to the broader concept of social capital. According to Ball (2008: 155), 'The extent to which people feel part of strong, social and community networks can best be encapsulated in the term "social capital"'. This can be defined as 'features of social life, networks, norms and trust that enable participants to act together more effectively to pursue shared objectives ... Social capital, in short, refers to social connections and the attendant norms of trust' (Putnam, 1995: 664–5). Investment in social capital by governments, particularly in areas of social and economic deprivation, should enable the individual to gain access to a range of opportunities otherwise denied to them, as well as the ability to benefit from them. It has to do with the 'material and immaterial resources that individuals and families are able to access through their social ties' (McNamara Horvat *et al.*, 2006: 457).

Investment in social capital is underpinned by a belief that it can, at least in part, explain class differences in relation to educational attainment. Whereas middle-class parents may be able to access and use resources available to them within their social networks to make informed decisions, working-class parents are less likely to have such resources available to them, nor the ability to make best use of them if they do. Targeting the child within its immediate network of family and community opens the possibility of breaking the cycle of deprivation and economic disadvantage. One way of investing in social capital is to invest in education and the concept of life-long learning as a vehicle for improving the opportunities available to disadvantaged communities and thus changing the life-chances of the most vulnerable children and young adults within those communities.

This was precisely the focus of policy-making for New Labour who made 'compensatory measures' a particular feature of their education policy (Lupton, 2006: 654). Tomlinson (2005) lists a number of early initiatives that were directed at tackling exclusion and minimising economic inequality. These include the Green Paper, *Excellence for All Children: Meeting Special Educational Needs* (DfEE, 1997), a simplified Code of Practice for SEN in 2001, a New Deal for 18–24 year-olds (1997), a National Childcare Strategy and the beginnings of *SureStart* in 1999. Furthermore, 'locating the areas or "zones" where the unemployed and disadvantaged were concentrated quickly became a major policy focus' (Tomlinson, 2005: 107). Five Employment Zones were identified in 1998 and the first of 25 Education Action Zones became operative in September of that year (ibid.). *Excellence in Cities* (DfEE, 1999) sought to 'improve parental confidence in the capacity of inner city schools to cater for ambitious and high achieving pupils' (DfEE, 1999: 1), a measure to improve trust and strengthen parent–school partnership.

Partnership is fundamental to the concept of new public management (NPM) – the delivery mechanism for many of the policy reforms described above. It serves as one method of breaking the power of professionals within the various sectors and promoting partnership and social cohesion. It is about tightening government control at local level. Social capital theory is one way of explaining class differences; it also explains social diversity and cohesion. The underlying assumption of New Labour's social policy was that education is the route out of poverty. Blair first announced his ambition to eradicate child poverty 'within a generation' (Blair, 1999) and Gordon Brown continued to pursue the halving of child poverty by 2010 and its complete eradication by 2020.

As we have already seen, the rhetoric of choice, competition and raising standards has framed policy-making since 1997. Neo-liberalism, the perceived benefits of a free market, business models and practices have assumed new levels of significance and import. Education and health are about 'delivery', 'accountability', 'choice' and 'standards'. The benefits system is about mobilising the unemployed to take responsibility and invest in education, training and skills. Good leadership and management are seen as signifiers of success.

Conclusion

The political, social and economic context in which *Every Child Matters* emerged points to a planned and strategic delivery of a wider social and economic policy agenda, set in motion immediately after the 1997 General Election. By centring the new social agenda around the child and family, New Labour was able to tackle, not only the highly emotive and contentious issue of child protection and wellbeing, but also some of the other key areas of concern for western governments at the end of the twentieth century. These will be dealt with in more detail in Chapter 2. In summary, New Labour was anxious in the first instance to open up the education sector further to market forces and private investment. It was the means of limiting the control and influence of professionals and enabling government to promote its own aims of social reform. The government was also keen to develop the new public management systems that would promote public participation and the adoption of government policy at local level. In effect it shifted the responsibility for perceived problems and threats from central to local government. Whereas it can be argued that children's health and economic or material wellbeing have improved over time, this is not the case for *all* children, nor has it necessarily been sustainable for others. The new social agenda was about investing in social and human capital in order to break the repetitive cycle of deprivation and to bring about sustainable generational change for the ultimate benefit of the state.

Chapter 2

Modernising the welfare state

New public management

Education and social reform

The outworking of current government policy across the areas of family, community, citizenship and social values represents a reconceptualisation of the relationship between government and the governed. Historically education has been one of several mechanisms for social reform with varying idealisms emphasising 'citizenship', 'social service' and 'character' (Harris, 1992). Examples of these are the education reports and policy which followed the two world wars or periods of economic depression and social unrest. The Newbolt Report (HMSO, 1921) looked into the teaching of English, both language and literature, and its role in forming cultural knowledge and experience. English language was seen as a means of 'saving the nation's children from poor speech habits' (Beverton, 2001: 128) and of finding 'a bridge across the chasms which now divide us' (HMSO, 1921, cited in Beverton, 2001: 129). The Butler Education Act (1944) divided children according to the type of education supposedly best suited to their future roles in the workplace: grammar school, technical school or secondary modern. Callaghan's Ruskin Speech (1976) questioned the progressive teaching methods in primary schools and demanded a closer link between the aims of education and the needs of industry. Similarly, the 1988 Education Act further tightened the link between education and work by introducing a national curriculum of skills and knowledge deemed essential for the economic future of the nation (Coulby, 2000).

The pace of change since 1997 has been significant and in itself forms a fundamental part of the discourse of the 'Third Way' politics described in Chapter 1. The plethora of reform emerging from the Blair Governments since 1997 served two purposes:

- to open up education to market forces and private investment as a means of limiting the control and influence of professionals over delivery (provider capture);

- to develop the creation of new public management (NPM) which promotes public participation.

Dale and Robertson (2008) argue that provider capture, the control of education by professionals rather than consumers, provided the stimulus for the creation of NPM and the creation of new relationships with government. Weakening the grip of the professionals within education served to open up education to market forces and to strengthen government control. According to Tolofari (2005), the link between NPM and governance is strongest where governance has to do with the structure of government and the setting up of strategy, while new public management, as opposed to 'old' public administration, is concerned with delivery. An example in education is the local management of schools on managerial principles and the heightened influence of stakeholders such as parents, governors and private investors, on the daily life of schools. The rationale for this has been identified as fivefold: economic, political, social, intellectual and technological (Tolofari, 2005).

According to Lauder (1991) theories of public choice, together with those of individual freedom such as Hayek (1960/1991) and market theories of provision and consumption based on competition, are underpinned by an assumption that individuals are 'rational egoists' and fundamentally concerned with the pursuit of self-interest. It is in the market-place that individuals have the freedom to best pursue their self-interest. However, in the political arena the pursuit of self-interest can lead to socially and economically undesirable consequences. Where education is politically controlled, rather than open to the influence of market forces, it is less likely to produce optimal outcomes. This interplay and subsequent tension between government, professionals and the market is at the heart of 'Third-Way' policy-making.

In *Every Child Matters* the expectation is that all agencies to do with child welfare, education, health, youth offending and social services work together. This multi-agency 'resectoralisation' – the removal of traditional sector barriers – enables the breaking down of existing 'provider' strongholds such as the trade unions and professional associations, thus facilitating the strengthening of government control.

New Labour's 'Third Way': Neo-liberalism/ post-modernism

According to Blair (1998, cited in Olssen *et al.* 2004: 200) the politics of the 'Third Way' unites two key themes characteristic of left-of-centre thought: democratic socialism (social justice with the state as the main agent) and liberalism (primacy of individual liberty in the market economy). In policy terms this translates into four distinctive stances:

- Economy – acceptance of fiscal disciplines together with investment in human capital, science and knowledge transfer;
- Civil society – a rights and responsibilities approach, strong on law but with social programmes to address the causes of crime;
- Public services – investment to ensure equality of opportunity but also restructuring to provide more individually tailored services built around the needs of the modern consumer, and to secure the public good that markets left to themselves could not provide;
- Foreign policy – robust on defence but committed to global justice.

Blair (ibid.)

Clarke and Newman (1997) argue that it is managerialism that typifies the central thread of changes over the last two decades, especially in terms of the state and the remaking of state institutions. To focus purely on social policy is to miss the wider agenda of modernising government and the restructuring of the state itself beyond its welfare functions (1997: 19).

The 'Third Way' is characterised by new roles of governance and a fundamental shift in the role of the state. Rather than promoting a strong centralised state which had been a feature of neo-liberal politics of the 1980s, the role of the state under New Labour was that of the 'enabling state' in which citizens at a local community level take an active part in running their own lives. Giddens (2000, cited in Olssen *et al.* 2004) argues that in order to be effective this must be underpinned by a level of social cohesion, sustained by a flourishing civil society. It calls for not only a new relationship between the individual and the community, as Giddens has argued, but also a new relationship between those individuals, communities and the state itself.

It is upon this new relationship that current education and child welfare policy is constructed. Moore (2004) argues that education is treated as a principal means of creating a more 'equal' society. The post-modern definition of educational outcomes is differentials in socio-economic advantages and disadvantages between groups. Changing the forms of schooling changes their effects, and consequently their outcomes. *Every Child Matters* is premised on the belief that education is the prime means by which children can be raised out of poverty. The focus is not so much on the advantages accrued by the individual child, but rather on the family unit as a whole, supported by a benefits system, and a belief in 'family learning' through the extended schools agenda. These measures fit with what Moore describes as 'external accounts' of that which is considered educationally significant in explaining the problems of difference: social background or genetic constitution. 'Externalist' accounts are principally concerned with deprivation theories and compensatory education. Schools are intended to make up the perceived deficiencies in the home or community. Examples of strategies to counter social exclusion are the *Head Start* project in the USA and, in the UK, the Education Action Zones (EAZs) later subsumed into the EiCs (Excellence in Cities) initiative and the *Sure Start* programme. The role of the 'enabling state' is to facilitate communities with local initiatives to target those families who have traditionally failed to equip their children to benefit from the school system.

Restructuring the state

The social policy encapsulated in *Every Child Matters* is part of a broader political agenda which seeks to redefine the role of the state and the mechanisms of power to meet the national, international and global demands of the twenty-first century. Fundamental to this process is the shift from hierarchies of government administration to networks. It allows for more focused government (Parker and Gallaher 2007), especially in a culture where resources are limited. This 'new organisational settlement' is structured around the mechanisms of managerialism and marketisation, and has led to the emergence of various tensions in Government policy. Examples are evident within *Every Child Matters*:

- education as the route into work and out of poverty, versus the reality of pay/status, especially for those who make up the children's workforce;
- parents viewed as the cause of welfare problems, versus parents as the solution;
- children enjoying and achieving at school, versus increased accountability for children and parents alike, testing, standards and the raising of the school leaving age.

In turn this has determined which groups will be disaffected: those social and ethnic groups, immigrant families and travellers who are on the margins of society.

In redefining what government should and should not be expected to do, responsibility and accountability have been removed from government to the market, to individuals and to families as a way of breaking the cycle of dependency and promoting initiative and choice (Clarke *et al.* 1998: 381). It is where families and communities 'fail' their children that they become the focus for state intervention. As such the state can define notions of good parenting, responsible citizenship and active participation and will set the standard below which children and families are deemed to be at risk.

However, nation states, especially western democracies, increasingly have to look to international comparisons such as the recent UNICEF *Report Card* (2007) to gain any real insight into the effectiveness of their social reforms. This report makes uncomfortable reading for the USA and the UK who found themselves at the bottom of the ranking of 21 industrialised nations. The report looked at child wellbeing across six dimensions: material wellbeing, health and safety, education, peer and family relationships, behaviours and risks, and young people's own subjective sense of their own wellbeing. In total, 40 separate indicators of child wellbeing – from relative poverty and child safety, to educational achievement and drug abuse – were brought together to give a relative overview of the lives of children. Northern European countries dominated the top of the table, whereas the UK came in the bottom third of five out of the six dimensions reviewed. Only in the educational wellbeing dimension did the UK rank any higher.

Changes in governance

These changes in the role and responsibilities of government have led to changes in governance. It could be argued that the focus of this change still remains at the level of processes and outputs reminiscent of Rustin's (2004) criticisms of the Laming Report. *Every Child Matters* can be viewed as the government's means of addressing urban disadvantage, promoting social cohesion, raising educational standards and continuing the drive for modernising public service provision. The shift from the old order of public administration to new public management has had an impact on traditional notions of social and cultural values, understandings of citizenship and the concept of responsible parenting. Under the new social settlement it is the responsibility of the individual to make the right choices and to behave 'properly', yet with increased accountability for those who fail. However, the reality of active public or community participation appears less positive than the rhetoric. Parents and other members of the community have so far had little engagement with the decision-making processes or management in their own community resources such as *Sure Start* children's centres. This is indicative of the ambiguities still to be resolved about the role of the citizen in government policy: whether they are deemed consumers of, or partners in, this new system of social welfare.

Redefining the education sector

Historically, education has been a conduit of social policy and change, and the current body of *Every Child Matters* legislation continues the tradition. At one level all policy can be said to address government fears and concerns and reflects the social, political and global contexts of the day. *ECM* challenges accepted understandings of education and the role of educators. Teachers have always had concerns for the whole child, but it was not the responsibility of education to address the complex needs of children at risk. Once identified, responsibility for the needs of such children would be passed to the relevant agencies. Under *Every Child Matters* it has become the responsibility of education in partnership with other agencies to provide dedicated support, not only for these particular children, but also for their families. One vehicle for this is the extended schools initiative. Under the Children's Trust arrangements and the Ten Year Strategy (DfES, 2004c) education took responsibility for the whole child from birth to the end of formal schooling. Schools became strategic in their connectedness with parents, families and communities; schools acted as the universal service for children. This altered the perceptions of educationalists' roles and allowed them to make more public commentary. It was headteachers who were amongst the first to voice their support for the director of Children's Services in Haringey in November 2008 following the 'Baby P' case, although Baby P himself was not of school age.

A single integrated inspectorate was constructed in 2006, retaining the old title of 'Office for Standards in Education' with the adjunct of Children's Services and Skills. This suggested a wider role for education. This broader inspectorate, together with the Healthcare Commission and the Chief Inspector of Constabulary, were called in to investigate the role of agencies following the 'Baby P' case with its uncanny similarity to the Victoria Climbié case. This was compounded in June 2007 by the creation of two new departments to replace the DfES: the Department for Children, Schools and Families (DCSF) and the Department of Innovation Universities and Skills (DIUS). DIUS was merged into the Department of Business, Innovation and Skills (BIS) in June 2009.

The DCSF was to lead in creating coherence for children, schools and families across Whitehall, securing improvements for all children, whilst closing the gap between the most disadvantaged and the rest of society. It was to break the cycle of deprivation for the most disadvantaged groups and to facilitate generational change. *Every Child Matters* advocated the local interpretation of a national policy framework through the work of local authority children's trusts which 'bring together all services for children and young people in an area underpinned by the Children Act 2004 duty to cooperate, to focus on improving outcomes for all children and young people' (DCSF, 2009a) and through the extended schools initiative in promoting and being accountable for the five outcomes.

Conclusion

Although *Every Child Matters* is ostensibly about the child rather than institutions, the underlying political motivation has more to do with a wider political agenda: that of redefining the role of the state through the restructuring or modernisation of governance. This, by definition, has to do with the institutional change evidenced in the Laming Report (HMSO, 2003) and the government's response. The blurring of boundaries between agencies and the breaking down of traditional sector-based professional or 'provider' strongholds serves to strengthen state control in these areas and subjugate their aims to those of government, while appearing to give more autonomy to local networks and communities. Herein lie the tensions evident throughout *Every Child Matters* and which are inherent in New Labour and 'Third Way' politics: social policy and neo-liberal market forces.

Chapter 3

International comparisons

No Child Left Behind and *Excellence for All Americans*

Introduction

Every Child Matters has its antecedents in the American policy *No Child Left Behind* (*NCLB*) (US Department of Education, 2001) produced by the Bush administration in 2001. This is one of the most important pieces of US Education legislation in the last 40 years. Like *ECM*, it was intended to tackle the effects of poverty and underachievement. What was new for Americans was that it extended central government 'federal' power over what traditionally has been a deregulated schooling system. By following the Bell and Stevenson (2006) framework for policy analysis outlined in Chapter 1, this chapter will show the similarities between American and British society in the impact of neo-liberalism and the weakening of the state. The political expedient was to introduce a national policy that focused on improving productivity as a response to economic globalisation and competition. Education is seen as a way of improving economic growth through greater alignment with the needs of industry and investment in human capital. It is also seen as a way of lessening the impact of poverty, social deprivation and inequality through the acquisition of training, skills and high-waged employment.

Context

No Child Left Behind represents the 42nd amendment of the Elementary and Secondary Education Act of 1965. This marked the beginnings of active involvement by federal government in education in the USA. As elsewhere in the western world, the USA has long been concerned with perceived underachievement, especially in relation to international comparisons such as the First International Maths Study (FIMS) (IEA, 2007) of the 1960s in which US pupils did badly. This, in the aftermath of the launch of Sputnik by the USSR in 1957 and the failure of the USA to be first in the space race, meant that schools were under pressure to raise standards. They needed to improve the uptake of mathematics, science and language courses in order to compete for supremacy in the new technological space-age.

Historically, the UK and the USA had achieved a high level of industrialisation in the nineteenth and early twentieth centuries. While their economies were flourishing, political control of education was minimal as there was no *economic* requirement for a formally educated workforce. However, as the industrial base gave way to modern technological and service industries in a globalised economy, so the demands on education changed. Productivity and economic competitiveness in the new world order became important and education was seen as the key to success. Brown and Lauder (1997) identify two political models emerging from the new right agenda of the late twentieth century. The first is 'neo-Fordism' characterised by market flexibility, a reduction in the power of trade unions, privatisation of public utilities and the 'rolling back' of the state. It is this model that the two governments have followed since the late 1970s with the policies of New Right Conservatism under Margaret Thatcher in Britain and Republicanism under Ronald Regan in the USA. A connection was made between increased spending on social welfare systems, high inflation, unemployment and economic recession. The answer was to impose market conditions, competition and managerialism as a way of improving standards and productivity. In the UK particularly, education was opened up to the market by extending parental choice. The political imperative was to increase the economic competitiveness of the workforce. The legacy, however, has been a polarisation in wealth distribution between the richest and poorest in society. Britain and the USA have become amongst the most unequal societies in the Western world (James, 2007; Wilkinson and Pickett, 2009). The professional middle classes have been able to perpetuate their investment in human capital, and the benefits that accrue from this, through the exercise of school choice at the expense of the poor.

The second political model is the centre-left 'modernisers', typified by New Labour policies in Britain and Democratic policies in the USA. Ideals are again based on assumptions about the global economy, skills and education, but they emerged as a left-wing response to the New Right neo-Fordist model. Old socialist strategies are regarded as no longer effective in the pursuit of social justice and economic efficiency. Instead modernisers are committed to investment in human capital and the economy to create a high-skilled, high-waged 'magnet' economy based on partnership between government, employers and workers (Brown and

Lauder 1997: 179). There were protective measures against exploitation, such as a minimum wage and support for low-income families through tax credits.

It is against this political and economic backdrop in the USA that *NCLB* must be viewed. The Elementary and Secondary Education Act (ESEA) of 1965 marked the beginning of active federal involvement in education with the aim of improving educational standards. Some twenty years later the Republican Regan administration published a damning report on education standards, *A Nation at Risk* (NCEE, 1983), which was to establish federal interest in school accountability, testing and choice. This culminated in the 42nd amendment of the ESE (1965) Act – *No Child Left Behind* (*NCLB*) in 2001 under another Republican President, George Bush.

The *NCLB* is first and foremost an education policy, but with new right (neo-Fordist) socio-political ends. Discourse is primarily about 'standards', and target-setting which became the familiar framework for educational improvement in the UK. Prior to 2002, individual states in North America varied in their approach to standardised testing, school improvement and accountability systems, in spite of various measures to bring them into line. For example, 'America 2000' (US Department of Education, 1991) and 'Goals 2000' (US Department of Education, 1994) provided grants to help individual states to develop academic standards. By 1994 the Reauthorisation of the ESE Act declared a nationwide commitment to standards-based reform. Congress adopted the notion of 'adequate yearly progress' (AYP) which was later to become the linchpin of *NCLB* (Rudalevige, 2003). Some states, such as Iowa, proved resistant to developing standards. Texas, on the other hand, embraced such measures wholeheartedly, developing a system of sanctions and rewards for schools (Thrupp and Hursh, 2006). The Texas Assessment of Academic Skills model became the blueprint for *NCLB*.

> *NCLB* received overwhelming congressional support when it was passed into law in January 2002. Its aims are compelling:
>
> - to provide better, more demanding education for all students;
> - to have all groups of students in every school move steadily toward a high level of achievement. Specific goals include:
> - improving early reading instruction;
> - upgrading the quality of teachers in high poverty schools;
> - providing information for accountability and improvement;
> - and setting the goal that all groups of disadvantaged students make

- substantial progress every year in every school;
- students in seriously failing schools should have an opportunity to go somewhere else;
- low-income parents to have resources to supplement their children's education.

(Orfield, 2004: 1)

To this end all fifty US states were to develop and conduct standardised testing in reading and maths for pupils in grades 3–8 in order to ensure schools make 'adequate yearly progress' (AYP). This was to be extended to include grades 9–12 with the addition of science testing by 2008. The act made available federal funding to areas and social and ethnic groups with a view to equalising educational opportunity for the most disadvantaged. Schools in receipt of such funding had to put in place standards for improving student achievement year on year, and produce detailed plans outlining how standards will be monitored and met. Particular attention had to be paid to the various subgroups within school populations who have traditionally underachieved – those from low socio-economic backgrounds, ethnic minorities or with English as an additional language. Scores were to be made public. For some schools this meant generating and reporting on the sores of numerous subgroups, which were then compared with the State's testing requirements to determine whether adequate yearly progress had been achieved (Thrupp and Hursh, 2006). If any one group failed to meet the required targets the entire school was designated as failing. The ultimate aim of monitoring and testing was to ensure that all students, regardless of gender, race, ethnicity, ability, or economic circumstance met minimum standards (100 per cent proficiency) by 2014.

The concept of testing and accountability was not new in the USA, but *NCLB* introduced stringent sanctions to the American schooling system. The threat of punishment and the loss of the best students were to be the incentives to drive up school improvement. Over time, the sanctions became more severe for any 'failing' school unless improvement could be demonstrated. Schools failing to make AYP for two consecutive years were classified as 'in need of improvement'. By the fourth year failing schools must either:

- replace school staff,
- implement a new curriculum,
- decrease management authority at school level,

- appoint an outside expert to advise the school,
- extend the school day, or
- reorganise the school internally.

Failure to improve after five years resulted in the school being restructured as a *charter school* (a privately funded public [state] school similar to the UK academies), all or most of the relevant staff being replaced, or the handing over of management to the State or a private company. Similar sanctions were applied to failing school districts.

Consequences

Critiques of *NCLB* indicate a number of consequences for this managerialist approach to school improvement which have resonance in the UK. *NCLB* has extended federal control of education and, in particular, has brought the curriculum within its remit. Whilst there is still no national curriculum within the USA, *NCLB* dictates that curricula must demonstrate 'effective, scientifically-based instructional strategies and challenging academic content' (NCLB Act, 2002, Title I, Section 1001 [9]). Ellis (2007) argues that this has limited the choice of curricula for teachers to that offered by providers who have won state approval. Ellis also comments on the competition which this has generated between publishing houses to produce scientifically-based curriculum materials, resulting in these publishing houses exerting undue influence on curriculum development.

Secondly, *NCLB* fundamentally changed the relationship between federal government and educators. Orfield (2004) suggests *NCLB* demonstrates limited understanding of the reality of schools or of the basic traditions of federal-state and professional relationships. There was an underlying assumption that schools themselves could tackle the problems of educational achievement for disadvantaged groups within a short space of time, and that there are known methods of reform to achieve this.

Thrupp and Hursh (2006), like Ellis, point to the narrowing and simplifying of the curriculum which has emerged from the drive to demonstrate raised test scores, particularly in urban districts. Teachers are compelled to teach the skills and knowledge that will be tested ('teaching to the test'), neglecting more complex aspects of a subject and even removing some subjects altogether, including the arts and sciences (Thrupp and Hursh, 2006: 650). The focus becomes passing the test, not the ability to apply knowledge in real-world situations. Subjects that are not tested, in the early grades for example, are in danger of no longer being taught. This narrowing of the curriculum has also been evident within the UK system since the introduction of SATs testing.

The introduction of sanctions led to the widening of parental choice and involvement in schools. Parents of students in those schools considered 'in need of improvement' may transfer them to another public school with transportation provided by the failing institution (Thrupp and Hursh, 2006). Those who remain are offered additional (private) tutoring. Parents can review and comment on the choice of curriculum offered by the school board and have the right to opt out of units of study which they object to within the confines of the law. Some subjects such as health, American history and science are state requirements. As experience in the UK has demonstrated, it is parents with greater access to information and higher levels of education themselves who are able to take advantage of such choice.

Finally, *NCLB* has been accused of widening rather than narrowing the socio- economic gap in spite of its directing of funding to areas of disadvantage. Ellis (2007) highlights the predicament of those schools and districts that do not have sufficient local funds to add to federal funding to sufficiently cover testing and curriculum costs. Thrupp and Hursh (2006) suggest that an emphasis on test preparation is likely to result in schools devoting much of their curriculum budget to test preparation materials rather than enrichment resources. Orfield (2004) also points to the financial crisis that hit some states following the first year of implementation. Promised resources were not forthcoming and it was the urban schools that were hit hardest. States kept back 20 per cent of federal funding to enable failing schools to pay travel costs or supplementary support, further disadvantaging those schools.

There is an apparent correlation between successful schools and family income. Most failing schools in New York, for example, were found to be in poor urban school districts. This is not surprising if all subgroups of the school population have to demonstrate improvement on all tests. Poverty, ethnic diversity and multilingualism militate against success. Narrowing the curriculum and teaching to the test further disadvantage such pupils, particularly if the knowledge and skills required to pass are not transferable outside school. Those pupils just falling short of minimum standards receive additional support, whereas Thrupp and Hursh (2006: 651) suggest that some schools force weak students out of school before taking the required exam or they are kept down, typically in the 9th grade. Students repeatedly 'kept down' are likely to become disillusioned and drop out. The net effect is to widen the gap between the socio-economic classes, rather than to tackle the causes of underachievement. Target-setting linked to punitive sanctions, according to this critique, perpetuates inequality and disadvantage rather than offering a solution.

Conclusion

There are profound differences between *NCLB* and *ECM*, not least because *NCLB* is primarily an education policy directed at raising educational achievement across the board, but with particular reference to minority groups. It has focused attention on underachievement, especially where associated with low income, ethnic background, special educational needs (SEN) and English as an additional language. It offers the potential for longitudinal data-collection relating to these subgroupings and the prospect of more systematic intervention programmes at school level. The burden of responsibility is firmly placed on education to raise achievement, whilst failing to take into account that minority groups are not evenly distributed throughout states and schools, but, as in the UK, are concentrated in particular urban areas. There is no concept of value-added measures familiar in the UK that acknowledge degrees of progress, even if levels fall below expected national standards. Under the *NCLB* framework for achievement, the low base of some of the most disadvantaged means they have to make greater progress year on year, and this perpetuates the inequality of educational disadvantage. As such, *NCLB* demonstrates the tensions between local (state) interpretation of the act and federal idealism. Individual states can set their own targets and standards, albeit within a centralised system of accountability, funding and sanctions. Conversely, *ECM* is primarily a social policy that has adopted education as its main conduit for change. It takes a more holistic view of the child, beyond levels of attainment, and in so doing widens the responsibility of schools to include the family and community contexts. *ECM*, via the *Sure Start* model, targets areas of disadvantage rather than individuals and allows for value-added measures that acknowledge the impact of schooling and intervention on progress, even if the raw scores in attainment tests fall below national standards.

NCLB and *ECM* represent policy responses to the New Right, neo-liberal agenda. They both focus on outputs (standards) as opposed to inputs (processes) which links to managerialism and accountability. There is an acknowledgement that local solutions are the best method of achieving centralised goals. In terms of *NCLB* this is about schools and school districts tackling underachievement. In *ECM* the philosophy is far more explicit and forms part of the wider agenda of modernising government and services via new public management. The impact of marketisation is evident in both systems with greater accountability, together with the development of parental choice, which serve to create a corresponding widening of the socio-economic gap. Above all, both *NCLB* and *ECM* mark a change in the relationship between government and education professionals, fuelled by a desire to roll out 'good practice' models into a coherent centralised system of reform that tackles issues of educational attainment among the socially disadvantaged.

Chapter 4

Sure Start

Combating urban disadvantage

Background to *Sure Start*

Sure Start began in January 1999 as an early-years intervention policy in each of the 20 per cent most deprived neighbourhoods in the United Kingdom. The aim was to raise the social, cultural, human and economic capital of the children and families with the Sure Start Local Programmes (SSLPs). Strategically, the initiative represents the notion of 'focused government' policy, promoting collaboration between government and local communities in targeted areas. 'Governments can focus their delivery systems on a relatively small number of particular goals through concerted periods of political prioritisation, policy development and implementation' (Parker and Gallagher 2007: 157). To this extent, *Sure Start* can be seen as a pilot for the wider *ECM* agenda, modelling approaches to public participation and multi-agency working. It also adopted an 'ecological perspective' on the trajectories of young children in line with Bronfenbrenner's (1979) Ecological Systems Theory.

Sure Start aimed to address both the systematic failures of the past in child protection and wellbeing and the state's need for more effective governance in the public sector. This is evident in the subsequent structural changes across government and local authority departments to accommodate new and collaborative ways of working. It involved public, private and voluntary sectors, and the approach was to identify and target specific communities, rather than individuals, for intervention. It has been described as 'a radical cross-departmental strategy to raise the physical, social, emotional and intellectual status of young children' (Glass, 1999: 257). Significantly the programme originated as a Treasury response to public spending, emerging from one of several cross-departmental reviews (e.g. Health, Education, and Home Office) which followed New Labour's election in 1997. The main thrust of the programme was to target families of children under four years of age living in areas of deprivation, and to address social exclusion through investment in human, social, cultural and economic capital. This was structured around the provision of better access to early-years education, healthcare, family support and advice via the local programmes (SSLP). In line with new public management these centres were locally led and managed, bringing together partnerships across public, private and voluntary agencies. The aim was to build on services already available in local communities and to offer an integrated approach to service delivery. Core services were identified as:

- outreach services and home visiting;
- support for families and parents;
- good quality play, learning and child care;
- primary and community healthcare and advice about child health and development;
- support for those with special needs.

(Glass, 1999: 258)

Local communities could also respond to local need by offering additional services: for example, training for parents in key skills such as ICT, personal development courses and practical advice and support, including debt counselling, literacy or language training.

The initial *Sure Start* programme rolled out in 1999 should not be viewed in isolation. It represented one of several strategies devised by government to focus on the needs of young children and their families. These strategies involved a drive to improve service provision and support for families, including the establishment of the National Family and Parenting Institute and the extension of free nursery places for all four-year-olds. Improved financial support for families was also targeted through the Working Families Tax Credit and the Childcare Tax Credit so that the tax system itself could be more responsive to the needs of those on low incomes. Above all, the drive to encourage families into work was argued for in the adoption of the European Union Working Time Directive, improved paternity leave and the development of a National Childcare Strategy.

Sure Start Local Programmes were part of a wider government strategy to tackle social disadvantage and they were to operate alongside the newly created Health Action Zones (HAZs), Education Action Zones (EAZs) and the New Deal for Communities (NDC). These initiatives, introduced during the first New Labour government (1997–2001), represented an early commitment to changing the role of governance from the old-style 'top-down' model of public administration to the 'partnership/network' model of new public management. Traditional sector boundaries become blurred in the interests of collaborative 'joined-up' working. These early initiatives should be viewed as pilot projects for exploring alternative mechanisms for effective service delivery. Terms such as 'trailblazers' or 'pathfinders' were attached to them and they were accompanied by plans for extensive evaluation so as to inform future practice and policy-making. HAZs were eventually incorporated into Primary Care Trusts and the EAZs were transformed into Excellence in Cities (EiC) action zones or Excellence Clusters.

Sure Start was influenced by five key discourses associated with the EAZs and cited by Power *et al.* (2004: 457) in their evaluation of the EAZ initiative:

- *Combating urban educational disadvantage*: discussions around egalitarian philosophies aimed at restoring issues of equality and disadvantage in education to the public arena;
- *School effectiveness and improvement*: academic–professional discourses emphasising ways in which good leaders can improve schools in any social context. In relation to *Sure Start* this would translate into developing and improving early years education;
- *New partnerships/joined-up action*: practical arguments for collaboration and multi-agency partnership informed by communitarian ideas or concepts such as 'social capital' and social exclusion;
- *Managerialism/modernisation*: debates which emphasise a range of managerial techniques for the governance of welfare. Central to this discourse was a concern to secure improvement by tying resources to outcomes that had to be continuously monitored;
- *Privatisation/marketisation*: a discourse which emerged from neo-liberal and Conservative policies of the 1980s and 1990s. Extensive privatisation was denied by the architects of the EAZs, while marketisation and private sector involvement was accepted as a necessary feature of the modern public sector.

Sure Start had at its heart the desire to combat urban disadvantage and to break the cycle of deprivation for young children and their families. It was about achieving sustainable generational change through the offer of good quality early-years education, family support, employment advice and healthcare delivered by professionals and experts in the field. In order to minimise the associated stigma of targeting individual families which characterised programmes of the past, whole communities became the targets for government intervention and monitoring. These were by and large the communities that failed to attract private investment in early-years provision when the sector was opened to market forces during the 1980s and 1990s and resulted in significant gaps in provision. The adopted agents for change within *Sure Start* were public/private partnerships which were able to encourage community involvement at project level, whilst demonstrating multi-agency working across the key sectors of health, education and social services. In this way *Sure Start* demonstrated the ability to bring in private investment to communities where market forces had failed. Furthermore, the operational expedient of bringing a range of services together under one roof was intended to be responsive to families with complex needs by offering a simplified system of referral and support. Although operating at a distance, levels of centralised control were high and monitored through the processes of accountability, inspection, and regular evaluation – the hallmarks of modernisation and managerialism.

The evidence base for early intervention

In many ways *Sure Start* and the subsequent introduction of Children's Centres stand in a long tradition of interventionist social policy. Moss (2004) identifies three key assumptions that underpin *Sure Start*:

- *the modernist idea of prevention,* with children as the principal target of prevention. Investment in children today will solve the problems of society for tomorrow;
- *a belief in the unique influence of the early years.* Applying powerful human technologies to children below a certain age will help cure social and economic ills;
- *a belief in the cycle of deprivation. Sure Start* aims to break the cycle of deprivation and exclusion for the whole generation of children currently living in poverty.

(Moss 2004: 632–3)

Early childhood intervention programmes have historically tried to improve children's health and development (physical, social and cognitive) as a means of addressing gross inequalities for children. Early intervention is generally understood as targeted provision over and above that which is normally available for families of very young children in any community. Services are offered in addition to the normal pre-school or health support provided for the age group. An example of such an early intervention programme was the introduction of the health visitor service offered to mothers of newborn babies at the beginning of the twentieth century. This was to address concerns for the physical conditions of the working classes in the growing industrialised towns of late-Victorian and early-Edwardian Britain. More recent targeted early intervention programmes in the UK include the PEEP programme (Peers Early Education Programme) of 1995, the National Family Literacy Programme introduced in 1996 and the Parenting Early Intervention Programme in 2008.

One of the largest and better known intervention strategies in recent history was *Head Start* implemented in the USA in 1965 and expanded by the introduction of *Early Head Start* some 30 years later. This federal programme targeted low-income families of pre-school children from the age of four, whilst *Early Head Start* was directed at children from birth to three. *Head Start* provided the model upon which *Sure Start* was based. The aim of *Head Start* was to narrow the attainment gap between children living in social and economic deprivation and their peers at the point of starting school, by focusing on their social, emotional, health and psychological needs (Gray and Francis, 2007). *Early Head Start* shared this focus of social, emotional and cognitive development, but looked to support parents with their child-rearing role and in achieving economic success. These elements are included in the UK *Sure Start* model.

Lessons from research on social intervention

After 40 years, *Head Start* has been evaluated by several longitudinal research studies which have generally been positive and suggest some long-term beneficial effects on participants. Evaluations of *Early Head Start*, which include family learning programmes, have also indicated benefits for parents and children. However, the Gray and Francis (2007) review of early intervention programmes suggests a number of cautionary lessons to be learned from the US experience.

Early childhood interventions can make a significant difference to children's life chances. However, expansion without funding threatens quality and the UK government planned for sustained increases in funding. At the outset, *Sure Start* received some £540 million and was set to expand to 500 local programmes by 2004 with a total investment of £760 million for the period 1999–2004. An additional £435 million was committed over 2003–2006 for the development of children's centres with the aim of opening 2,500 centres by 2008 (Moss, 2004: 631). SSLPs all became *Sure Start* children's centres and there were to be 3,500 by 2010.

Narrower objectives which are easy to measure can crowd out broader objectives which are more complex. Whether the programmes reach the families for whom they are intended and are effective for them is a case in point. Children's centres represent the original *Sure Start* principles of integrated service delivery and support of parents and young children, but were required to operate under tighter performance regimes and guidance on what was to be delivered and how. From 2006, children's centres came under the control of local rather than central government. Programmes were to balance adherence to the generic model with flexibility to local conditions. High levels of centralised control and inspection can result in standardisation and uniformity across the service, whilst limiting responsiveness and risk-taking to meet the needs of users at local level.

Multiple objectives may conflict. The intervention was designed to target improvement in terms of health, education, social welfare, family support and employability. The National Evaluation of Sure Start (NESS) monitored implementation, impact, local context and cost effectiveness. Conflicts were found in:

- selectivity versus universality;
- locally expressed need versus central government determined need;
- the needs and rights of children versus those of parents;
- evidence-based rather than entitlement-based services.

(NESS, 2005)

Programmes may have differential impacts. This will be dependent to a large extent upon uptake and use, as well as the nature of those availing themselves of the services on offer.

What are the benefits?

The sustainable benefits of early-intervention programmes are less easy to quantify. One major concern of such programmes is whether they reach the children and families for whom they are designed. This is a particular cause for disquiet in the modern approach to targeted provision where whole communities rather than individuals become the focus for implementation. In the interests of removing the potential for the stigma attached to services directed towards individual families, more generalised programmes may fail to meet the real needs of their target users. Uptake of the programme cannot assure participation by those for whom the programme is intended. This is particularly so in relation to early-years provision which is not statutory. Participation in pre-school services is voluntary and more likely to be made use of by those already investing in human, social or cultural capital, rather than by those with the most limited resources. However, it cannot be assumed that refusal to participate is necessarily a negative response. Some families may actively reject such provision for reasons which do not reflect anything untoward about the family or the services on offer. On balance, however, evaluations of initiatives such as *Sure Start* have to question whether the notion of the 'hard to reach' family is indeed accurate, or whether it is the service provision that is hard to reach. Offering a service to everyone within a needy community may, without due care, limit accessibility to those in most need.

Hannon *et al.* (2008) discuss the success of *Sure Start* in terms of 'reach' which they define as 'contact' and 'use'. 'Contact' refers to what programmes do to meet their responsibility to maximise families' access to services through advertising and open days. 'Use' refers to whether, and to what extent, families take up the services offered in a programme (p. 210). Of course, the uptake of services in a voluntary programme will depend on family choice and the nature of the services on offer.

Bronfenbrenner's Ecological Systems Theory

Locating *Sure Start* within targeted communities is fundamental to the programme and is based on underlying assumptions about children, families and the wider communities which exert influence upon them. Bronfenbrenner's (1979) Ecological Systems Theory provides a useful model for understanding the influences on child development and interaction. The model locates child development within the context of a complex system of relationships in the child's immediate environment. Human development takes place through these progressively more complex and reciprocal interactions between the child's bio-psychological make-up and the 'persons, objects and symbols in its immediate environment' (Bronfenbrenner, 1994, reprinted in Gauvain and Cole 1993: 38). The immediate environment is made up of family, community and the larger society. The ecological environment is conceptualised as a 'set of nested structures', each inside the other which Bronfenbrenner likened to a set of Russian dolls. Each level impacts the other and the overall development of the child who is located at the centre:

- Microsystem: Immediate environments such as family, school, peer group, neighbourhood, and childcare;
- Mesosystem: A system comprised of connections between immediate environments such as a child's home and school;
- Exosystem: External environmental settings which only indirectly affect development such as parent's workplace; and
- Macrosystem: The larger cultural context, national economy, political culture.

(Evans *et al.*, 2007: 1)

Bronfenbrenner's later work included what he described as the 'PPCT model' of development. This consists of processes (interactions), the person, context and time, and the interrelations between them (Trudge, 2008: 67).

Ecological models have helped in the understanding of the processes and conditions that define human development and explain the disparity that exists in the trajectories of certain groups of children. This is particularly evident in relation to the impact of social, economic or cultural status on the outcomes for children. Early intervention programmes such as *Sure Start* are a way of minimising the negative impacts of low socio-economic status on children and families. By conceptualising the child at the centre, the ecological model allows for focused and systematic intervention across the child's immediate environment where negative impacts on development can be identified. It therefore becomes possible to measure the impact of poor housing, generational unemployment, bilingualism or low levels of parental education on child development. In this way the rationale for early intervention becomes self-evident.

Evaluations: Has *Sure Start* worked?

If the intention of Sure Start Local Programmes and the subsequent *Sure Start* centres was to combat intergenerational disadvantage by investment in early years, then it has been important for government and stakeholders to be aware of the impact. We saw earlier that the unique feature of the *Sure Start* early intervention programme was that it was an area-based rather than 'user-targeted' initiative. According to those involved in the National Evaluation, this has called for a distinct approach to the research methodology following what they call an *'intention-to-reach'* design (Belsky and Melhuish, 2007: 133). They argue that an area-based intervention will have both direct and indirect effects on children. Direct effects are those derived from the use of services such as speech therapy or good-quality childcare. Indirect effects on childcare are mediated either through parents and parenting or through the community. These have sometimes been described as 'ripple effects'.

The NESS Impact Study relating to children and their families focused on four key areas:

1 Did children/families in SSLPs receive more services or experience their communities differently?
2 Did families function differently in SSLP?
3 Did effects of SSLPs extend to children themselves?
4 How did effects on children come about?

(Belsky and Melhuish, 2007: 148–9)

Findings indicated that there was little evidence that SSLPs achieved their goals of increasing service use or of improving families' impressions of their communities. They did appear to improve family functioning to a degree, especially amongst non-teen mothers of 36-month-olds. For children from relatively less disadvantaged households there was some benefit to be derived from being in an SSLP area. This was not evident for those from more disadvantaged families such as teen mothers, lone parents or workless households. Instead, they appeared to have been adversely affected by living in an SSLP community (Belsky and Melhuish, 2007: 149).

Rutter (2007) has offered a useful evaluation of *Sure Start* and the accompanying research. The programme differed from previous interventions in five key respects:

1 It was explicitly designed to be area-based to provide a service for seriously disadvantaged communities. Those communities were to decide for themselves what was required. Participants were to 'buy-in' or opt into the programme rather than have services externally imposed. Not all deprived families live in areas of deprivation and would not benefit from targeted provision.
2 *Sure Start* began with no deliberate specification of how goals were to be met or what type of curriculum was to be offered. Again, this was left to the local areas to decide.
3 There was a lack of emphasis on professional skills, supervision or detailed monitoring.
4 Unlike most major research studies of interventions, the piloting of the project did not occur before it was rolled out, even though it had been argued for.

5 An implicit assumption was that SSLPs would improve overall parenting functioning as well as improve child development. Evaluations of the New Zealand experience demonstrated that, although child-related outcomes were good, more general benefits in family functioning were not evident, and yet the expectation for SSLPs to achieve this remained.

Rutter acknowledges the government's recognition of, and commitment to, early-years intervention by investing new money into the *Sure Start* project, allowing for the transformation of services in the UK for pre-school children. However, the UNICEF (2007) report did not set the UK in a good light with respect to services beyond pre-school, indicating the high levels of teenage pregnancy and the low levels of young people in education beyond 16. The importance of the early years, according to Rutter, is that early experiences tend to shape later life, not that they reflect any 'critical periods' in child development (cognitive, physical, social or emotional).

Rutter is most critical of government expectations of *Sure Start*. Statements lacked both 'consistency and precision' (2007: 199). One objective was to improve conditions for young children; yet a repeated emphasis was placed on the role of SSLPs in tackling child poverty and social exclusion, a focus that has not insignificantly continued through the *Every Child Matters* agenda. Families differ in their ability to take up and benefit from services, depending on their resources; so it is highly likely that universal interventions such as *Sure Start* can increase rather than reduce social inequalities. In terms of child poverty, although this has reduced, the government did not meet its five-year target (Commission on Families and the Wellbeing of Children, 2005, cited in Rutter, 2007). This reduction has more to do with the alterations in the benefits system than with opportunities offered through the SSLPs. Moving families from no employment to the minimum wage does not lift a child out of poverty. Implementation of the programme was poor and the government failed to use the best research designs or to respond to initial findings. In 2006 they altered the remit of the SSLPs, turning them into children's centres answerable to local government. This appears to be more in line with the political agenda for promoting *ECM* rather than developing lessons from a new model of intervention. Questions of sustainability and levels of actual community involvement remain.

Chapter 5

The five outcomes

A social agenda for the UK

Introduction

This chapter explores what constitutes the norm for children today and the perceived threats to their quality of life and opportunities. The analysis is based on the Thomas and Hocking (2003) report for the think-tank, Demos. The report examines how children's quality of life is changing and might be improved. Three social trends are identified:

1 Risk aversion – the tension between the adult's 'guardian' mentality and the desire to give the child the freedom to learn;
2 Colonisation – intensive adult-based supervision of children which may reduce a child's quality of life;
3 Commercialisation – the rise in children's spending power that makes them targets of commercial pressure.

The five outcomes of the education system: to know how to be healthy, stay safe, enjoy and achieve, make a positive contribution and achieve and maintain economic wellbeing, are examined against this background. The outcomes represent the government's formulation of its objectives for British society as a whole in raising the cultural, social, economic and human capital of those to whom *ECM* is directed. They encapsulate the New Labour government's responses to perceived threats to their status and power at local, national and global levels.

The Demos report (2003): *Other People's Children*

Thomas and Hocking identify the government's agenda for children since 1997 as twofold: creating 'ever higher, safer and more stringent standards for individual children, while attempting to recoup the deficit for children "at risk"' and emphasising the need for early investment. The latter has been demonstrated through government investment of new money in *Sure Start*. However, they contend that this, and the alternative 'children's rights' movement, may fail to reach all children and will 'entrench compartmentalised responsibilities for children's lives, encouraging a blame-and-compensation culture' (2003: 13). Children's experiences of, or status and influence in, society may not be improved.

The UK Government signed up to the United Nations *Convention of the Rights of the Child* (UNCRC) in 1991. Forty-one of the 54 articles refer to the human rights of the child often clustered together under the categories of the 3 Ps (Isles, 2008):

- provision to ensure children's survival and development (welfare rights);
- protection from abuse and exploitation (welfare rights);
- participation in decision-making (liberty rights).

Through the 2004 Children's Act, and in the development of the *Every Child Matters* five outcomes, the UK government tried to ensure the participation of children and young people in the services that affect them and that their voice was both sought and heard. The five outcomes themselves were derived from consultation which included children and young people; the appointment of the four Children's Commissioners across the UK was another way of promoting children's voice.

However, the way children and childhood itself are perceived dictates the manner of response. Welch (2008) identifies a number of trends here: that children are viewed by adult society as 'vulnerable or victims', as against children being 'capable or villains'. Childhood can either be seen as 'important in its own right' or as a 'preparation for adulthood'. The view that children are 'vulnerable' is particularly powerful and has led to the social trends of risk-aversion and colonisation mentioned above. Of course, the vulnerable need protection, yet over-protection can limit a child's freedom and the ability to learn how to manage risk for itself. Hence, school playgrounds are out of bounds during times of heavy snowfall in case children fall and hurt themselves, or the traditional game of conkers is banned for similar reasons. Fear of litigation and the predominance of a blame culture is also a part of risk aversion. The experience for the majority of children is to be under constant adult supervision and it has become the exception rather than the norm to find children playing freely in open spaces. This has threatened the adult–child relationship in the wider community in that children are no longer expected to view adults as responsible and helpful, but as a potential menace and threat, even though most child abuse or abduction occurs within the close family network. 'Stranger danger' has also made adults, particularly men, question their public and social responses to children. There is now uncertainty as to whether it is appropriate to approach a lost or distressed child.

The aim of the Demos report was to examine such changes in the quality of children's lives in the twenty-first century and to look for ways it could be improved for all children over the next generation. The purpose was to challenge current discourses surrounding children and to look for a framework for tracking and improving quality of life. The emphasis on quality of life is significant and, as the report highlights, stems from dissatisfaction with measures of economic growth and income as indicators of child wellbeing (Thomas and Hocking, 2003: 10). Quality of life is determined by a combination of complementary states:

- individual standard of living;
- shared resources;
- happiness and emotional wellbeing;
- trust and inclusion.

Using this framework for analysis significant trends are identified in the report:

1 Children's life chances in terms of medical health, financial wellbeing, educational achievement and personal safety have risen enormously over the last generation. However, this is against a backdrop of rising individualism to the extent that quality of life is more directly linked to parental income and earning power. For poorer families the wider costs of individualism are clearer: the ability to pay for childcare, the cost of travel to visit dispersed family members and the lack of play facilities compensated by 'individual' toys such as PlayStation.
2 Children's psychological development, emotional resilience and mental health. Although the report asserts that findings are mixed, the research does indicate that life has become more emotionally demanding for children. Incidence of major life changes such as divorce, house moves and changes in childcare together with greater exposure to media of different kinds are cited. Although families may have adapted in developing more open forms of communication with children, other institutions such as education and commerce have not been so adaptive, placing children under pressure to achieve higher academic standards and consumer expectations.

3 Children's dependence on social capital and informal gift exchange. This is an area considered in the report to be poorly researched. Thomas and Hocking suggest that, for a number of reasons including risk aversion, children are in danger of becoming segregated from other aspects of community life. This threatens their childhood experience, but also their profile and influence in wider society.

The report argues that the response to such change has encouraged fragmentation, so that different sectors in society have taken responsibility for different aspects of children's lives. For example, retailers and corporations seek to 'give children what they want', while governments focus on minimising harm and promoting child protection. The media represent the child at risk, whereas charities campaign for children's rights. The role of government in all this could be to iron out the obvious inconsistencies and create manageable and accessible pathways for children and parents. However, government is struggling with low levels of trust in itself, and in the public sector staff recruitment and retention in children's services, particularly social work, is reaching crisis point. This is further exacerbated by cases of child abuse and neglect gaining national media coverage.

However, Thomas and Hocking (2003) propose a strong link between 'neighbourliness' and children's wellbeing. This resonates with Putnam's discussion of 'social capital':

> For a variety of reasons, life is easier in a community blessed with a substantial stock of social capital. In the first place, networks of civic engagement foster sturdy norms of generalized reciprocity and encourage the emergence of social trust. Such networks facilitate coordination and communication, amplify reputations, and thus allow dilemmas of collective action to be resolved. When economic and political negotiation is embedded in dense networks of social interaction, incentives for opportunism are reduced. At the same time, networks of civic engagement embody past success at collaboration, which can serve as a cultural template for future collaboration. Finally, dense networks of interaction probably broaden the participants' sense of self, developing the "I" into the "we," or (in the language of rational-choice theorists) enhancing the participants' "taste" for collective benefits.
>
> (Putnam 1995: 66)

One interesting critique of current civil society is the 'ethics of care' which offers to counter the trends identified above and links with Putnam's view of collaborative networks (Held, 2006). This works on the principle that people are 'relational' rather than 'self-sufficient individuals'. One contended view of society, prevalent since the 1980s, is that it is made up of independent, autonomous units who cooperate only when cooperation affords mutually positive ends for those parties, the view held by Margaret Thatcher, noted in Chapter 1, that 'there is no such thing as society' (*Woman's Own,* 1987). Values such as independence, non-interference, fairness and rights are dominant. However, the ethics of care in Held's view sees people as relational and interdependent in 'the moral claim of those dependent on us for the care they need' (2006: 10).

> 'Moral emotions' (sympathy, empathy, sensitivity and responsiveness) are valued and the moral claim of the 'particular other' is respected, even though this can create tension between 'care and justice, friendship and impartiality, loyalty and universality'
>
> (ibid.: 11).

That people can think and act as if they were independent depends on the network of social relations established from childhood. Therefore, many of our responsibilities are embedded in familial, social and historical contexts (Held, 2006). The onus is on individuals *taking* responsibility, rather than the individualist view of tolerance and 'leaving each other alone'.

Of the recommendations in the final chapter of the Demos report, the priorities are first to give children the vote, and second to align the age of majority to the age of criminal responsibility at 14. Families should decide how to use that vote until the age of majority is reached. Emphasis also is given to the need for a national play policy to increase the opportunities and accessibility of play and learning for children in all communities. Demos calls for an annual survey from leading charities to review the range of risks to children's wellbeing in order to promote strategies for communicating and reducing such risks. Without a collective response in similar vein to Held's view of interdependent social relations or Thomas and Hocking's notion of 'neighbourliness', attempts to improve children's quality of life will be limited. However, it would appear that it is individualistic rather than collective ideals that are promoted through the *ECM* outcomes.

The five outcomes

The inference from the *ECM* five outcomes detailed below is that certain groups of children do not enjoy or sustain these states of safety or wellbeing. Chapter 10 deals with the responsibilities devolved to parents by government in ensuring these outcomes for their children. The focus here is on the underlying perceptions of children and childhood, and the values and norms being promoted by government. There is a tension between government intervention (or interference and coercion) and the

Table 5.1 The ECM five outcomes

Be healthy	
	Physically healthy
	Mentally and emotionally healthy
	Sexually healthy
	Healthy lifestyles
	Choose not to take illegal drugs
Stay safe	
	Safe from maltreatment, neglect, violence and sexual exploitation
	Safe from accidental injury and death
	Safe from bullying and discrimination
	Safe from crime and anti-social behaviour in and out of school
	Have security, stability and are cared for
	Enjoy and achieve
	Ready for school
	Attend and enjoy school
	Achieve stretching national educational standards at primary school
	Achieve personal and social development and enjoy recreation
	Achieve stretching national educational standards at secondary school
Make a positive contribution	
	Engage in decision-making and support the community and environment
	Engage in law-abiding and positive behaviour in and out of school
	Develop positive relationships and choose not to bully and discriminate
	Develop self-confidence and successfully deal with significant life changes and challenges
	Develop enterprising behaviour
Achieve economic wellbeing	
	Engage in further education, employment or training on leaving school
	Ready for employment
	Live in decent homes and sustainable communities
	Access to transport and material goods
	Live in households free from low income

DfES (2004d: 5)

right of individuals and children, young people and parents to exercise their own choices and values within the law.

The details of the outcomes imply a deficit model of childhood which requires government intervention. There is an assumption that children and young people are both vulnerable to, and victims of, adult society, including the family and community with whom they are associated. They are to make appropriate choices and to be encouraged to do so by the family and teachers; 'choose not to take illegal drugs'; 'choose not to bully and discriminate'; 'attend and enjoy school'; 'engage in law-abiding and positive behaviour in and out of school'.

Protectionist values are promoted through safeguarding; children are to be safe from 'maltreatment, neglect, violence and sexual exploitation'; 'accidental injury and death'; 'bullying and discrimination'; 'crime and anti-social behaviour'; 'they are to live in homes free from low income'. Indeed some of these statements also indicate a view that children and young people themselves are part of the problem, and that their behaviour needs to be curbed. They are to engage in 'law-abiding and positive behaviour'; 'engage in further education, employment or training on leaving school'. Failure can result in fines for parents when children fail to attend school or, since 1999, the issuing of an anti-social behaviour order (ASBO) applicable to children as young as ten years of age.

There is also evidence that childhood is seen as a preparation for adulthood, and not a respectable status in its own right. Statements in the section on making a positive contribution and achieving economic wellbeing are pertinent here: children and young people are to 'engage in decision-making and support the community and environment'; 'develop self-confidence and successfully deal with significant life changes and challenges'; 'develop enterprising behaviour'; 'be ready for employment'. These are to be encouraged through the outworking of the citizenship curriculum at both primary and secondary levels.

The outcomes impose middle-class expectations and values upon certain groups of children and young people. Measuring wellbeing has proved notoriously difficult and is highly subjective; a parent's or a teacher's view of child wellbeing may be very different from that held by the child itself. UNICEF (2007) and Barnardo's Scotland (2007) each used different domains of wellbeing, as did Bradshaw *et al.* in the *Index of Child Wellbeing in the European Union* (2007). The DCSF measures child wellbeing against the five outcomes. The Welsh Assembly and the Northern Ireland Assembly use different indicators. In other words, measures of child wellbeing are, in Bradshaw's words, 'multi-dimensional'.

Above all, the five outcomes are about interventionist strategies to promote social norms. Under the current Ofsted inspection regime, schools are measured on how far they contribute to achieving the five outcomes – what measures they have in place for ensuring a child's health or safety or how far they are developing social and academic skills in preparedness for employment. This fits with the government commitment to generational change. It is about investment now for benefits far into the future.

Conclusion

Through the UNCRC the state has responsibility for upholding the rights of the child, as do parents and carers. This, however, can present tension between the need for state intervention where appropriate and the perception of state 'interference'. The dilemma is faced daily by those working with children and families 'at risk'. *ECM* has marked a significant shift away from the old 'protectionist' models of the 1945 welfare state to one of emphasising the need for preventative measures and services. Rather than removing children from families, social workers in the famous 'Baby P' case of 2008 claimed that the pressure was to keep children with their parents wherever possible. This principle is upheld in the Progress Report of March 2009 (Laming, 2009) and, for the majority, this has to be right. Knowing when and how to intervene has to be made clear for all parties. Deficit models of parenting and childhood implicit in the five outcomes do not reflect the complex lives and values of modern children, but rather demonstrate the New Labour government's social agenda for good behaviour, good parenting, and good communities producing educated and productive citizens. In the final analysis the outcomes for children are not ultimately designed for the wellbeing of the child, but as preparation for a productive adulthood in the global economy.

Chapter 6

Poverty and economic wellbeing

Introduction

The common features in the redesign of welfare regimes in Britain encapsulated by *ECM* are human capital, investment for the future and life-long learning. The underlying political belief was that there is a cycle of deprivation that ensnares children and young people and limits their life chances and opportunities. According to New Labour rhetoric, this had to be tackled for two main reasons: to secure an educated workforce for a competitive knowledge economy and to minimise the risk of social exclusion with its consequences for children and young people. The focus was not so much on the advantages accrued by the individual child or young person, but rather by the family unit as a whole and the community in which it is situated. Children are self-evidently 'symbols of the future' and the goals and outcomes set for them are by necessity for the long term.

The tools with which New Labour sought to redesign the welfare system were the adoption of targeted intervention, an integrated approach to service provision, the establishment of clearer lines of accountability both locally and nationally, and the enforcement of parental responsibility and support. Overall, this marked a significant shift in the emphasis for provision from protection to prevention. This chapter explains the nature of these concepts. It explores some of the economic changes that preceded *ECM* and which underpin its agenda. Factors that influence economic wellbeing, such as poverty and social exclusion, are discussed.

The problem of poverty

Whereas industrialised nations in the latter half of the twentieth century have experienced high economic growth with improvement in standards of living, child poverty has remained persistent. Indeed, several western industrialised nations, including the UK and America, have had to grapple with the re-emergence of high levels of child poverty in more recent years (Vleminckx and Smeeding, 2001: 1). The key contributors to this were the steep rise in earnings inequality caused by neo-liberal economic policies (see Chapter 1) throughout the 1980s and 1990s and the consistent rise in the numbers of lone-parent families.

According to recent figures from the Joseph Rowntree Foundation (JRF):

- The proportion of children living in poverty has doubled in the past generation.
- The UK has proportionally more children in poverty than most rich countries.
- In 2006/7, 2.9 million children were living in poverty.
- 600,000 children were lifted out of poverty between 1998 and 2006.
- This compares with a government target of 850,000 to be lifted out of poverty by 2004 and 1.7 million by 2010.
- In addition to the human cost to families and children of allowing high levels of poverty to continue [...] research estimates that child poverty costs £25 billion each year in costs to the Exchequer and reduced GDP.

(Joseph Rowntree Foundation, 2009, emphases original)

In 1999 at the Beveridge lecture, Prime Minister Tony Blair announced his commitment to halving child poverty by 2010 and eradicating it by 2020. This was followed by a number of interim measures aimed at reducing child poverty by a quarter by 2004. These were largely to be achieved by redistribution and reform of the tax system, targeting low-income families and encouraging saving. Although the target for 2004 was missed, the aim was laudable and directed attention and resources at the problem, including initiatives such as the welfare-to-work programme, the New Deal for Young People and New Deal for Lone Parents, the Working Families Tax Credit and the setting of a national minimum wage.

According to the Centre for Economic and Social Inclusion and the Child Poverty Action Group (2008):

> [t]his commitment grew from the recognition that the material circumstances into which children are born and in which they develop have not only short term impacts on their health and education but also impact in the longer term on their life chances as adults.

There is no single definition of poverty and it can be defined in terms of material, economic or social conditions. Conventionally, poverty is described as either *absolute* where basic needs such as clean water, food and shelter are not met, or *relative*. The UK Government has adopted a relative definition: that poverty is the relationship of an individual's standard of living with those around him or her.

> Poverty can be defined objectively and applied consistently only in terms of the concept of relative deprivation. [...] Individuals, families and groups in the population can be said to be in poverty when they lack the resources to obtain the type of diet, participate in the activities and have the living conditions and amenities which are customary, or at least widely encouraged or approved, in the societies to which they belong. Their resources are so seriously below those commanded by the average individual or family that they are, in effect, excluded from ordinary living patterns, customs or activities.
>
> (Townsend, 1979: 31, cited in Townsend and Kennedy, 2004: 10)

Furthermore, there are recognised types of poverty that affect households in the UK and, by default, children. These are commonly known as 'transient', 'persistent' and 'recurrent' poverty.

> Recurrent poverty reflects the fact that income mobility is short-range. Household income might increase enough to lift them just above the poverty threshold, but they remain on the cusp of poverty at high-risk of re-entering poverty. About 30 per cent of those leaving poverty re-enter again within a year and 30 per cent of the 'pool' of people in poverty over a six-year period were the same households moving in and out of poverty.
>
> (Smith and Middleton, 2007: 2)

Families move into poverty for a number of reasons, including changes caused by job loss or family constitution in the arrival of a new baby or divorce. More women than men suffer from poverty. Linked to poverty, but by no means synonymous with it, is the notion of social exclusion. The term gained popular currency in the UK during the 1990s and the establishment of the Social Exclusion Unit (SEU) appeared as an early reform in Blair's first government in December 1997. (It was closed in 2006.) According to the SEU's report of 2001 the Government defined social exclusion as:

> a shorthand term for what can happen when people or areas suffer from a combination of linked problems such as unemployment, poor skills, low incomes, poor housing, high crime, bad health and family breakdown.
>
> (Townsend and Kennedy, 2004: 12)

What is significant here is the recognition and understanding that these factors and their consequences are linked and thereby often highly complex. *ECM* assumes that *any* child or young person is vulnerable to the impact of such factors at *any* point in their lives. This is one reason why the policy agenda extends beyond the recommendations of the Laming Report (HMSO, 2003) with a focus on *all* children, not just those already deemed 'at risk'.

If defining poverty and social exclusion is complex, so too is the need for an accepted measure of poverty. Indeed poverty is, by its very nature, difficult to quantify; therefore poverty indicators are used as a tool for distinguishing the poor from the non-poor. Such indicators can be income-based, for example the World Bank uses a threshold of one dollar a day; or they can be budgetary, based on the cost of a minimum basket of essential goods. The EU adopts a comparative measure based on a line calculated at 60 per cent of the median income for each country. Nations with greater income inequality by this measure, such as the UK, have greater numbers of poor. In Britain this measure for poverty is only one of several adopted by Government and is published in the *Households Below Average Income* (HBAI) reports by the Department of Work and Pensions (DWP). The figures for 2007/08 indicate that:

> there were 2.9 million children living in UK households with below 60 per cent of contemporary median net disposable household income Before Housing Costs and 4.0 million After Housing Costs.
>
> (DWP, 2009)

Amongst those primarily at risk of poverty are children and the very young. Experience of poverty, especially recurrent poverty, is recognised as having enormous consequences for the life trajectories of children and young people:

> Poverty places strains on family life and excludes children from the everyday activities of their peers. Many children experiencing poverty have limited opportunities to play safely and often live in overcrowded and inadequate housing, eat less nutritious food, suffer

> more accidents and ill health and have more problems with school work. Much evidence exists of the link between growing up in a low-income household and experiencing a specific outcome, such as low educational attainment. Some children not only live in low-income families, but experience other poor outcomes, sometimes in combination with one another.
>
> (HM Treasury, 2004a)

New Labour and the promise of economic wellbeing

Poverty is a matter of policy-making, both in terms of its causes and the measures used to address it. Poverty reduces resilience to change and the ability to access services effectively. It is affected by where a family lives, changes in the industrial landscape which impact the economic climate and job prospects, and the make-up of the family. Families from minority ethnic backgrounds or with disabled members are more likely to be affected than other groups in society. As a means of addressing these issues *Every Child Matters: Change for children in schools*:

> sets out the national framework for local change programmes to build services around the needs of children and young people ... [to] ... maximize opportunity and minimize risk.
>
> (DfES, 2004a: 2)

It was through this programme of change to structures and procedures that the government aimed to improve the five outcomes of being safe, healthy, enjoying and achieving, making a positive contribution and enjoying economic wellbeing. These were outcomes that children and young people themselves identified as being key to wellbeing in childhood and in later life (DfES, 2004d: 4) (see Chapter 5). The programme was also aimed at '[narrowing] the gap between those who do well and those who do not' (ibid.: 4). Inclusion of economic wellbeing is integral to this process and points to the goal of long-term sustainable change for individuals, families and communities. The *National Service Framework for Children, Young People and Families* (DH, 2004) was considered integral to this process, setting out a ten-year strategy for improving children's health and wellbeing to be implemented via the primary care trusts (PCTs), local authorities (LA) and other partners. This was to align with the wider aims of the *ECM Change for Children* agenda. It set out eleven standards for the promotion, delivery and access of services across agencies, including schools, and made explicit expectations for both providers and service users. It covered pregnancy to adulthood and focused on:

- health promotion and prevention
- supporting parents
- integrated child and family-centred services
- growing up
- safeguarding children.

Indicators of economic wellbeing

The *ECM* framework of 2004 (DfES, 2004a) identified specific targets and indicators for each of the five outcomes. These indicated the government's key areas of concern and the targeted measures to address them. Targets, indicators and assessment criteria are made explicit. Those for economic wellbeing are given in Table 6.1.

The aims of securing economic wellbeing are closely linked to education and employment as well as publicly funded childcare to facilitate families into work. Significantly, achieving economic wellbeing is the only one of the five outcomes where the government identified no indicators. Only the Public Service Agreement (PSA) targets are listed. This could be because economic wellbeing is a long-term goal or because, like poverty and social exclusion, defining indicators of economic wellbeing can be elusive. However, the expectation that education, childcare and employment can work together to raise families out of poverty is explicit in the *ECM* documents. There is little regard for the number of working families still struggling below the poverty line. Access to paid employment does not necessarily mean poverty is overcome, even with a guaranteed minimum wage. The scale of the problem calls for more than a focus on investment in human capital through engagement with education and training.

Approaches to solutions: Economic wellbeing and the CYPPs

Fundamental to *ECM* and the reconstruction of the welfare state is the emphasis on local response to local need. Local authorities were charged with appointing a children's trust to address the fragmentation of children's services, strengthen accountabilities and construct a Children's and Young People's Plan (CYPP) for the area in consultation with children and providers. In 2006 the NFER published research based on the analysis of CYPPs across 75 local authorities. The aim was 'to build a

Table 6.1 Targets and indicators for the five outcomes of *ECM*

Outcome	*Aims*	*Support*	*Targets + monitoring body*
Achieve economic wellbeing	Engage in further education, employment or training on leaving school	Parents, carers and families are supported to be economically active	% of 16–18 year-olds not in education, employment and training – DfES
	Ready for employment	% of 19 year-olds achieving Level 2 in NVQ 2 or equivalent – DfES % of 18–30 year-olds participating in higher education – DfES	
	Live in decent homes and sustainable communities	% social housing and vulnerable households in the private sector in a decent condition – ODPM Cleaner, safer and greener public spaces, and quality of the built environment in deprived areas – ODPM	
	Access to transport and material goods	Level of material deprivation and low income – DWP	
	Live in households free from low income	% children living in low-income households – DWP, HMT Stock and take-up of childcare for all families – DfES, DWP	

(Adapted from DfES, 2004d)

national picture of the content of the plans and how they contributed to the five outcomes of Every Child Matters' (NFER, 2006: 1). The sample was representative of the types of LA whether county, unitary, London borough or metropolitan.

The findings of the NFER study in relation to economic wellbeing offer a way of understanding the ways in which LAs have interpreted this imperative and translated it into required actions, key groups and targets. Two priority areas were identified across the sample:

- education (post-16), employment and training (EET)
- standard of living.

Actions relating to EET tended to focus on curriculum development, post-16 provision for education and training, supporting young people's learning and decision-making, and education employment partnerships. The inclusion of higher education was noted as being less common in the plans. Actions for standard of living centered on the improvement of housing and transport for young people, and childcare and household/ family incomes for parents and families. The most frequently mentioned group was children with learning difficulties and disabilities (CLDD), with an emphasis on supporting their transition into post-16 and adult life. Looked-after children (LAC), including those leaving care, were also commonly identified with actions referring mainly to their housing and accommodation. Targets were seen as being predominantly numerical within EET, the most common relating to 16–19 year-olds not in education, employment or training (NEET) and non-numerical for standard of living (NFER, 2006). A recent OECD report indicated that the UK had more 'NEETs' than most other countries at 10.7 per cent in 2007. The international average was 7.2 per cent, putting the UK above Turkey, Israel, Brazil and Spain (Paton, 2009).

Significantly almost half the CYP plans across the sample of 75 explicitly identified a lead agent responsible for actions and targets such as Connexions, Education and the Learning and Skills Council, as well as the Children's and Young People's Service/Children's Trust (NFER, 2006) This typified the government's restructuring of welfare service provision and its emphasis on partnerships and networks for an integrated service delivery.

The role of education and economic wellbeing

Both government and local authorities identified education as playing a key role in achieving the outcome of economic wellbeing and moving individuals, children and families out of poverty. Investment in and expansion of education was the hallmark of New Labour policy. The result has been a reconceptualisation of the role of education, the nature of the education sector and the professional role of the teacher. High investment in pre-school provision and post-compulsory education has had a dramatic impact on the numbers of children and young people under the remit of education at any one time. Emphasis on life-long learning has also extended adult learning. Standards of attainment have risen, but the attainment gap in relation to social class remains persistent. Concerns that the widening of parental choice and a corresponding diversity in the types of schooling on offer has advantaged middle-class families at the expense of lower socio-economic groups are widely reported (Ward and Eden, 2009). However, what has shifted over time is the notion that education can only be successful in tackling disadvantage when working in conjunction with other aspects of the welfare system, including housing, employment and health. This calls for an integrated approach to policy-making and delivery. Allowing local authorities to respond to local need has the potential for making a difference with more targeted intervention, building on the successes of the *Education Action Zones*, *Excellence in Cities* and *Sure Start*. The inclusion of education within the 2007 *Children's Plan*, the extended schools initiative and the Education White Paper (DCSF, 2009b) continue to develop a wider vision for schools which goes beyond performance targets and exam results. The focus on targeted intervention for 'at risk' groups persists in more recent policy-making. For example schools are accountable for the progress of targeted groups such as looked-after children (DCSF, 2007a). Inevitably those schools in areas of disadvantage or with disadvantaged intakes bear the greater burden. Although government money is made available by way of ring-fenced grants, schools often have to bid for it on a competitive basis.

Conclusion

Herein lay the dilemma for New Labour: on the one hand embracing market strategies which perpetuate social divisions, whilst at the same time aiming for educational equality by attempting to narrow the attainment gap for low achievers as the means of achieving economic success and wellbeing. Education becomes the means by which human capital can be invested for economic productivity and employment at the risk of perpetuating social inequality and economic diversity. Knowledge becomes a commodity and education an investment with economic growth as the indicator of quality of life and wellbeing. However, there is a significant literature emerging which suggests the fallacy of such an argument: material income does not necessarily provide sustained improvements in wellbeing, and the whole notion of economic wellbeing is problematic.

Chapter 7

Child welfare and looked-after children

From protection to prevention

Introduction

Old protectionist models of child welfare provision in place since 1945 have been challenged under the *ECM* agenda and replaced by a more holistic system which takes a multi-dimensional/multi-agency approach to the complex needs of children, young people and families. Removing children from harm, whilst safeguarding the child, does not tackle the long-term social and economic causes of deprivation and abuse. Developing services around the child suggests opportunities for interventionist models that prioritise prevention over protection in relation to child welfare issues. The family and community around the child become the necessary focus in this alternative model. Recent policy takes the form of integrated, multi-agency working in order to address the call for 'joined-up', 'wrap-around care' which ultimately alters the relationship between families, service providers and the state. However, the changes to children's services encapsulated in *ECM*, including those for 'looked-after children' in the care of the local authority, have not occurred in a political vacuum. They are part of the reform of the welfare state and safeguarding system which can be traced back to the late 1960s. Such reforms reflect the rapid shifts and changes in modern society. The tensions in policy-making and service delivery are in the balances between:

- the role of the state in protecting children,
- maintaining the rights and privacy of the family, and
- acknowledging the rights of the child.

Community-based welfare and support

Historically state intervention in the lives of children had been the point of last resort, dominated by the principles of the Poor Law (1832, 1834, 1847) (Woodward, 1985). The Poor Law offered a system of relief to the poor, initially organised by parishes. The Poor Law Amendment Act in 1834 reorganised the system on a national scale, ensuring the building of workhouses in each Poor Law Union. The workhouse provided the key social benefits of shelter, food and labour (but not education) for those unable to support themselves, primarily widows, orphans, the sick and the elderly.

The construction of the welfare state begun by the Labour Government after the Second World War was to change that. Local authority children's departments were established in the 1948 Children Act to take over the responsibility of children in care, and were made accountable to the Home Office. There was a greater emphasis on foster care or adoption for children, rather than keeping them in residential institutions, and a belief that, where possible, children should be returned to their natural parents. Children in the care of the local authority were assumed to have the same needs of family, health and education as all other children. It became the role of state welfare to *support* those natural systems of welfare that were ordinarily located within the family. This reflected the social roles of the day, with male members being responsible for bringing in the family wage, whilst women were responsible for child-rearing and the wellbeing of all the family members. It was the role of the new children's departments to provide wherever this normal family-based welfare activity failed (1948 Children Act, Section 12, cited in Frost and Parton, 2009: 8).

By the 1970s the support role grew, with greater emphasis on working alongside families in the community in a preventative way, rather than waiting for families to get into difficulties and children needing to be taken into care. These reforms reflected contemporary professional and academic thinking which recognised the potential of preventative action as well as the links between 'child neglect, deprivation and delinquency' (Frost and Parton, 2009: 9). There was a growing belief that offering early intervention and support to families would have a positive impact on the numbers of children taken into care and their future outcomes. Local authority social services departments were established in 1971 following the Seebohm Report of 1968 and the Local Authority Social Services Act of 1970 creating 'a new local authority department, providing a community based and family-orientated service, which will be available for all' (Home Office, 1968, para 2). Professional social workers worked with families across all age-groups and the departments coordinated other aspects of state welfare such as health, housing, education and social security. Their task was to mediate and resolve the

> often ambiguous relationship between the *privacy* of the family and the *public* responsibilities of the state so that children could be protected and the privacy of the family was not undermined.
>
> (Frost and Parton, 2009: 11)

The emphasis in the Seebohm Report was the provision of services to the family. The committee rejected the notion of differentiated adults' and children's departments on the grounds that a single social services department would enable greater coordination, attract more resources and allow for more effective strategic planning and provision. Preventative action, research and community development were considered essential to effective service provision which was to be community based and responsive to local need.

The crisis in child protection

As mentioned earlier, such a community- and family-based approach was underpinned by certain beliefs and expectations of the family as an institution. However, by the end of the decade (1970s) there was a crisis in child protection and social welfare which reflected the wider political, social and economic crises of the times. The family could no longer be relied upon as a key instrument of welfare. The notion of family was changing with more liberal attitudes to marriage and divorce and the growing number of one-parent families. The traditional social roles defined by work and family were also under threat with the rise of feminism, demands for equal pay and growing unemployment through the loss of traditional manufacturing and heavy industries. Social welfare problems and their solutions were recognised as being far more complex than had once been understood. The need for change was reinforced by a number of high-profile cases and inquiries into child abuse during the 1970s and 1980s, e.g. Maria Colwell and Jasmine Beckford. The Maria Colwell case highlighted the tension between the rights of the birth mother and maintaining the family and those of the child. Maria, who had been fostered for five of her six years, was returned to her mother and step-father in 1971 only to die of neglect and physical abuse some fifteen months later (Hopkins, 2007). The public inquiry which followed was the first of its kind and pointed to

> poor communication and liaison between the agencies and a lack of co-ordination. Despite 50 official visits to the family from social workers, NSPCC inspectors, health visitors, police and housing

> officers, there was poor recording, a lack of information sharing, and a lack of any collation of case history.
>
> (ibid.)

Similarly, the inquiry into the death of four-year-old Jasmine Beckford in 1984 focused on the failure of agencies to communicate. It criticised social workers for 'regarding the parents of children in care as the clients rather than the children in their own right' (ibid.). According to the Department of Health and Social Security (DHSS) there were similarities in the findings across the inquiries into these cases. Frost and Parton (2009: 11) summarise these as:

- lack of interdisciplinary communication;
- a lack of properly trained and experienced front-line workers;
- inadequate supervision;
- too little focus on the needs of the child as distinct from those of the family.

These, and subsequent cases of child abuse and death, raised concerns that welfare professionals had failed in their obligation to protect the children in their care. However, where professionals attempted to be proactive, as in the Cleveland Affair of 1987 where over a hundred children were kept in hospital on suspicion of abuse and against the wishes of their parents, they were also in danger of criticism of being over-protective and over-reacting. The three-way tension between protection, prevention and the rights of the family was not to be easily resolved, and has been rehearsed once more in the public debates. The 'Baby P' case of 2009, in which an 18-month-old had been tortured to death by his mother and her partners, raised the public and media interest to a new level.

The Children Act (1989)

Politically, critics of the classic welfare state argued that it was based on what Dean (2003: 1) calls 'solidaristic' principles of collective responsibility which 'bred dependence' and fostered a 'dependency culture' where people ceased to observe the moral norms necessary for social order. The response of the New Right under Margaret Thatcher throughout the 1980s was to locate the responsibility back with the family, to attempt to 'roll back the state' to produce minimum state intervention and encourage a return to Victorian moral obligation and obedience (see Chapter 1). The 1989 Children Act made this particularly clear. The state should only intervene to safeguard and promote the welfare of the child and intervention should be the minimum required (Walker, 2008a: 139). Any intervention should be based on appropriate evidence that it is in the best interests of the child. The Cleveland Affair had suggested that children could be damaged as much by the interventions and investigative procedures of professionals as by neglect and abuse. The 1989 Children Act reinforces the belief that children are 'effectively the private property of parents and their welfare is only of concern to others if these parents fail to deliver safe outcomes' (Walker, 2008a: 140).

The fundamental principles of the Act are summarised by Walker (2008a: 138) as:

- the welfare of the child is paramount;
- parents have responsibilities as well as rights;
- the family (birth family or foster/adoptive) is the best place for children to live;
- children have the right to be protected from 'significant harm'.

Furthermore, Frost and Parton (2009) see the significance of the Act in terms of its principles of:

- negotiation
- partnership
- support
- and the broader power to provide services to *promote* the care and upbringing of children within their families.

This typifies the philosophy of the Thatcherite 'New Right'. Their ideas were based on the writings of the social philosopher Friedrich Hayek (1960/1991) who argued that the welfare state limited people's creative energy and produced, as in the title of his book, '*the road to serfdom*'. Thatcher's aim was to allow people greater control over their own lives.

The 1989 Children Act placed a new emphasis on local authorities to safeguard and promote the welfare of children and to provide a range and level of services appropriate to those children's needs (Section 17(1)). It provided definitions and criteria upon which state intervention could be based: if a child is or is likely to be suffering 'significant harm' understood as 'ill-treatment, or impairment of health or development'. Furthermore, there was an important shift in responsibility for local authorities to identify the life trajectories of children at risk: predicting what might happen to the child in the future.

New Labour and the modernisation of welfare

By the time the 1989 Children Act was implemented many of the key themes in New Labour's *Every Child Matters* and the 2004 Children Act were already in place. The response of the New Right to the criticisms of the classic welfare state had been to 'roll back the state' and encourage a return to moral obligation. The Third Way under Tony Blair and New Labour from 1997 sought to 'modernise' it. The aim was to develop an active rather than passive welfare state underpinned by notions of civic responsibility and self-governance. It was about investing for the future rather than compensating now. Services were to be preventative, promotional, positive and future-orientated. Children and families encapsulate these ideals and the communities in which they are placed were seen as a way of defining and addressing the complexity of social problems faced by them.

The modernising approach was heavily influenced by new public management (NPM). This looked to identify evidenced-based best value and best practice by setting performance targets, inspection and accountability regimes and in emphasising appropriate outcomes. The processes of modernisation included 'joined-up' policy and practice from government down to practitioner level, partnership and networking across professional sector boundaries, including the public, private and voluntary arenas and the use of modern information technology to improve efficiency. It was to this end that the spending review of 2002 *Opportunity and Security for All* (HM Treasury, 2002) looked at service provision for children 'at risk'. Their findings concluded:

> that despite extensive investment in services for children, most services are not having the desired positive impact on the most disadvantaged children. Key issues include insufficient local ownership by key agencies of the needs of children at risk, and the lack of a strategic vision pulling together the contribution of different local services and agencies to ensure that children receive appropriate support. The recommendations seek to ensure that support for children at risk is better focused on both preventative services and the preventative elements of mainstream services that address the known risk factors. These fall into three main areas: delivering sustainable services; improving strategic coordination; and filling gaps and improving services.
>
> (HM Treasury, 2002, para 28.4)

In order to improve strategic coordination the review recommended:

> better strategic planning; systematic identification, referral and tracking regimes to ensure children don't fall through the services safety net; and allocating responsibilities for individualized packages of support for those at greatest risk. The Government believes there is a case for structural change to effect the better coordination of children's services, and will pilot Children's Trusts which will unify at the local level the various agencies involved in providing services to children.
>
> (ibid., para 28.5)

Sure Start and the Children's Fund were introduced to address the need for 'prevention and early identification of need' (HM Treasury, 2004b, para 28.6) and to help meet the need for sustainable services. Furthermore:

> the review recommends the adoption of a common framework for integrating the lessons learned from successful programmes so that mainstream services are better able to respond to the full range of children and young people's needs on a fairer and more equitable basis. Within this framework the review recommended the following proposals to facilitate greater integration to meet the needs of all children:
>
> - multi-disciplinary working underpinned by core learning and skills objectives across all statutory and voluntary agencies; and
> - integrated service delivery and co-location of services to ensure better coordination, the maximum use of capital investment and support for 'mainstreaming' approaches.
>
> (ibid., para 28.6)

A 'national framework for improving the support that is available for parents and families at a local level' (ibid., para 28.7) using the voluntary sector as service providers was identified as a means of filling the gap and improving service provision.

Herein lies the blueprint for *ECM*. Although informed by the Laming Report (HMSO, 2003) into the death of Victoria Climbié, the Green Paper *Every Child Matters* continued the process of reform for children at risk already outlined in the 2002 Spending Review. However, the focus of the proposals was not merely the children at risk typified by the Climbié case, but was extended to *all* children, emphasising the belief contained in the Spending Review that:

> [c]hildren at risk do not form a self-contained, easily defined group. Many children and young people can be vulnerable to risk factors such as poor parenting, disability and poverty at some point in their development.
>
> (HM Treasury, 2002, para 28.3)

Education was identified as one of the key universal services alongside health that could deliver such preventative, promotional and future-orientated policy, as well as offering the infrastructure and manpower to do so. At Government level, overall responsibility for *ECM* was located within the Department for Education and Skills (DfES) soon to be restructured into the Department for Children, Schools and Families (DCSF). This restructuring of welfare provision for children at risk, and for all children, met New Labour's aim of reducing the perceived inadequacies of old state bureaucracies, limiting the power of professionals (provider capture) and drawing on much-needed private finance and expertise via partnerships and networks. What emerged was a wide-ranging social policy predicated on the belief that the whole workforce based around children, young people and families should be operating together to provide joined-up, multi-agency responses to the complex task of safeguarding children. English local authorities were restructured to combine social services and education departments into a common directorate of children's services. Structures were put in place to assist the integration process, namely a Common Assessment Framework (CAF) and the Information Sharing Index (IS Index), renamed ContactPoint in 2007 (DCSF, 2007a).

Education and children in care (CiC)

The safeguarding agenda has highlighted the shared responsibility of all agencies and government departments for positive outcomes for all children. Those who have been in the care of the local authority are of particular concern. Their vulnerability is unquestioned and poor levels of educational achievement seem difficult to shift. While many have had positive experiences of local authority care, this cannot be said of all children. Statistically they are more likely to suffer the effects of social exclusion in later life.

The most recent statistical data suggests that there were 43,700 children who had been looked after continuously for at least twelve months by English local authorities at 30 September 2008 (Statistical First Release, 2009). The outcomes indicators for these children make salutary reading. Thirty-three thousand looked-after children were of school age with 28 per cent having a statement of special educational need. Twelve per cent missed at least 25 days of schooling and 1 per cent received a permanent exclusion. Fourteen per cent who were looked after continuously for at least 12 months obtained at least five GCSEs or GNVQs at grades A* to C. This compares with 65 per cent of all school-children in year 11 who gained five or more grades A* to C at GCSE or equivalent (ibid.).

ECM has done much to raise awareness of the needs of children in care and yet as Kassem (2006: 170) observes 'the educational attainment of looked-after children is determined in most respects by two very different worlds'. This tension exists between the professional expectations of social workers and social services on the one hand and teachers and the education system on the other. Targets and workloads may obscure the discrete needs and priorities for children in care, although both services are working towards the same outcomes. This demonstrates the complexity of multi-agency working. Kassem has also observed:

> The key issues are that too many professionals, teachers and social workers locate the blame in the low educational attainment of looked-after children within the experiences the child went through before coming into care. That is in effect locating the problem with the child. The real issue is located within the system and attitudes of many who work with looked-after children.
>
> (Kassem, 2006: 171)

The Government White Paper, *Care Matters* (DfES, 2006a), attempts to address this. Children in care are given priority in school admissions arrangements, with an assumption that they will not have to move schools; they are given access to personalised learning support through a personal educational allowance of £500, better assessment and intervention and improved 14–19 provision. Also announced was targeted action on poor attendance and improved support for carers. From September 2009 all schools were to have a designated teacher responsible for children in care.

These proposals were taken forward with the publication of *Improving the Educational Attainment of Children in Care* (DCSF, 2009c). The strategy comprised three points of action:

- local authorities to have a virtual school head to track closely the progress of every CiC and ensure that they receive the support they need;
- every school to have a designated teacher to work with each child to plan to raise their attainment and respond to their needs, including providing one-to-one tuition wherever appropriate;
- local authorities to provide stable placements and schooling.

There is a strong emphasis here on the local authority and schools working closely and more effectively together. This in effect extends the corporate parenting role of the local authority as champion for the educational needs of children in care, and reinforces the notion of collective responsibility for children's wellbeing and positive outcomes enshrined in the *ECM* agenda.

Conclusion

This chapter has explored the role of the state in relation to child welfare and charted the various shifts in policy between protection and prevention. Fox Harding (1997, cited in Blewett and Foley, 2008: 180) has summarised these as:

- Laissez faire and patriarchy: the neo-liberal stance of rolling back the state, allowing for minimal intervention and underpinned by a traditional view of the institution of the family.
- State paternalism and child protection: the benign state protects and rescues children from inadequate parental care. This has in the past served to overlook the poor outcomes of children in care.
- The modern defence of the birth family and the parent's rights: a stance that also supports state intervention, but which should be supportive. The emphasis is on early intervention and preventative measures.
- Children's rights and child liberation: children are autonomous citizens with full civil rights. The emphasis here is on their perspectives, wishes and feelings.

The last of these will be discussed in the next chapter. What we have seen is a broadening of state responsibility towards children at risk which extends far beyond a need to remove them from harm, together with an extension of the notion of corporate parenting. The enabling state is now about removing, or at least minimising, risk factors through various processes of monitoring, target setting and early intervention. It is about encouraging corporate and collective responsibility through negotiation, partnerships and networks that cross sector boundaries, while emphasising responsibility and accountability. The use of electronic databases and information sharing has become integral to the multi-agency approach and the modernising agenda of New Labour. However, the enabling state is also about promoting positive behaviours and attitudes. This new understanding of safeguarding sees protection and prevention more as a continuum than alternative responses to the complex issues of securing child welfare and wellbeing.

Chapter 8

Citizenship and the new social order

New Labour, new social order

The new social order promoted under New Labour and encapsulated within *ECM* was constructed around a welfare system based on the assumption of gains to be accrued in the future. These gains are the child's and the later adult's wellbeing, but also the fitness to join the economic workforce. Present investment in that future is encouraged via community involvement, as well as in the acquisition of education, training and skills. Central to this new social order is the child:

- as part of a family in its wider, more liberal constructs;
- as a 'citizen in waiting';
- as an expression of cultural values and aspirations, defined by government and mediated through schools;
- in creating a rationale for greater social cohesion and community involvement.

Third-Way politics is characterised by the tension between a political imperative of centralisation in order to establish greater state control over key agencies such as education, and marketisation, which empowers the individual with choice, acting on the basis of personal self-interest (see Chapter 1). Local communities become both the cause of and the solution to the perceived breakdown of social norms.

Political focus has concentrated on notions of social cohesion, public participation, community regeneration, and citizenship as the means of addressing the rapid changes faced by western societies. This chapter explores understandings of civil society, community and active citizenship with reference to the works of Andrews (2004), Olssen *et al.* (2004) and Levitas (2005). Held's (2006) work on the 'ethics of care' and her understandings of the way societies and communities operate, also contribute to the discussion (see also Chapter 5). This is particularly apposite in a post-Christian era when traditional institutions such as the church and family can no longer be relied upon to define and promote 'national' moral and ethical values. Neo-liberalism has contributed to the rise and influence of individualism, which in turn has challenged social cohesion. Community, like citizenship, is multi-faceted and may no longer hold the same values or allegiances as those promoted by government.

Understanding citizenship

The effect of globalisation and political or economic migration means that western societies are no longer homogenous (if indeed they ever were), but rather are made up of a wide and diverse ethnic and cultural mix. This challenges traditional understandings of citizenship and national loyalties. Citizens are citizens on many levels. National or state loyalty is no longer a given. Furthermore, the lack of interest, or trust, in politicians and the democratic process has weakened the party mandate.

> [T]he last three decades have witnessed significant fluctuations in the percentage of people who voted in general elections. The turnout in the June 2001 election was the lowest since the election in 1918 (with none of the unusual post-war circumstances). Only 59 per cent of those registered turned out to vote in 2001 compared to 76 per cent in 1979. In the last election, 41 per cent of all votes went to the Labour Party.
>
> (Social Trends 32)

This has given rise to a renewed focus for government in defining what it means to be a responsible citizen and in encouraging active citizenship. Historically, education has been used, either directly or indirectly, as a means of promoting citizenship, particularly in the inter-war years in reaction to the horrors of the First World War and the fear of Fascism (Chitty, 2004: 180). Nevertheless, as Levitas (2005: 12) points out, 'citizenship ... is another word that can embrace many meanings'. Various models of citizenship have been put forward in an attempt to define the connection between individuals and the state. These necessarily have changed over time. Classical understandings of citizenship relate to the offer of the protection by the state in return for loyalty. There was a clear distinction between citizens and non-citizens. The Goldsmith Review (2008) of citizenship, however, demonstrates the complexities of the modern situation, which is linked to Britain's imperial past. This is compounded further by a perceived decline in national loyalty and attachment arising from globalisation and international interdependency. Heath and Roberts (2008) highlight the potential effect of declining national identity on society, citing Anderson's (1983: 6–7) view of the nation as a 'political community' defined as a 'deep horizontal comradeship' where nationality can become the basis of 'mutual obligations and social solidarity' (Heath and Roberts, 2008: 5).

Concerns about social cohesion were high on the New Labour agenda in 1997. The creation of the Social Exclusion Unit in 1997 demonstrated this political imperative. Constructing *ECM* as a social policy around the child legitimised government intervention in family and community matters. Targeting those sections of the population and physical geographical areas of the country that threatened social cohesion and were vulnerable to social exclusion allowed immediate needs in society to be addressed. Initiatives such as Excellence in Cities and *Sure Start* were further examples of the policy.

Under New Labour, citizens were considered to be stakeholders in society. They were *citizens* in so far as they voted in elections, *consumers* in their use of local services and *shareholders* in that they paid taxes (Gyford, 1991: 181). 'The rights and duties of stakeholder citizenship therefore focus on the types of stake each citizen has in the relevant aspects of the political process' (ibid.: 181). The notion of 'stakeholding', already well established in the management literature, had gained particular prominence in political discourse during the 1990s when the negative effects of capitalism and social exclusion were becoming evident. The notion of a stakeholder society and a stakeholder economy offered an alternative model 'where there is a mutuality of rights and obligations constructed around the notion of economic, social, and political inclusion' (Hutton, 1997: 3). Alistair Darling (1997: 10), a member of the New Labour government, argued that stakeholding was a 'straightforward political concept', which addressed two dominant facts of the age: a feeling of alienation from the political process and a growing sense of economic insecurity. He contended that the role of the state was to maintain an economic and social framework that would give individuals the opportunity to succeed. This was intended to produce a climate of stability and investment in a skilled workforce. People gained a stake in the country by engaging in paid employment. In Darling's analysis, stakeholding is about cultural change. It is both a government and individual philosophy, one that fosters partnership between the individual and the government which they elect. Employment becomes the dominant expression of an individual's stake in society.

There are tensions within the stakeholder view of citizenship. Andrews (2004: 2) makes the distinction between civic-individualism and civic-republicanism. Civic-individualism associates active citizenship with self-reliance and decreased dependence on the welfare state. Good citizens are consumers of public services. Civic-republicanism, on the other hand, associates active citizenship with direct participation in political decision-making. Good citizens are committed to individual and collective political engagement.

Furthermore, these arguments impinge on the discourse of personal choice. Under New Labour choice is realised through policy initiatives (Olssen *et al.*, 2004). It is presumed that individuals will make the best choices based on personal need rather than those offered by providers such as the state. Consumer choice is therefore more rational and better for both the individual and community and is thus regarded as a core value. Greater choice leads to greater equity and efficiency. Unbridled choice, however, is considered detrimental to social cohesion and community wellbeing. Olssen *et al.* (2004), like Held (2006), argue for localism as an effective model of public service provision. Localism is about the opportunity to give people greater ownership and control over the policies that affect their lives, increased civic participation and improved public services. It allows for new models of governance and public–private partnerships. Participation, facilitated at local level, enables self-government, which in turn springs from the notion of a strong and active 'enabling' state, co-opting citizens into running their own lives.

Citizenship education

Developing an active and responsible citizenry became an essential element in combating social exclusion, whist at the same time promoting the modernising of government through new pubic management at local, regional and national levels. Under New Labour it became the role of the state to ensure equality of opportunity and access to services for individuals. However, it did not guarantee equality of outcome. Responsibility lay with the individual to take advantage of the opportunities available to them and to invest in their social, cultural, economic and human capital for benefits in the future. Being a member of an active, participatory citizenship was one means of ensuring this. Putnam (1993) identified four key themes relating to the notion of civic community:

- civic engagement;
- political equality;

- solidarity, trust and tolerance;
- associations: social structures of cooperation.

This is about active participation in public affairs, equal rights and obligations for all, dialogue and respect. Such skills can be developed through engagement in civic associations and networks. To this end, citizenship education was formalised in the National Curriculum for England and Wales in 2002, and became compulsory for those wishing to gain UK citizenship from abroad. The changes to the national curriculum orders to incorporate citizenship education occurred followed the Crick Report in 1998. The aims of citizenship education were:

> to make secure and to increase the knowledge, skills and values relevant to the nature and practices of participatory democracy; also to enhance the awareness of rights and duties, and the sense of responsibilities needed for the development of pupils into active citizens.
>
> (DfEE and QAA,1998: para 6.6)

Citizenship education, compulsory at secondary level, falls within the remit of Personal, Social and Health Education (PSHE); at primary level it remains non-statutory although at the time of writing this is under review. The aims of citizenship education relate closely to the *ECM* five outcomes, especially that of *making a positive contribution*.

- Engage in decision-making and support the community and environment
- Engage in law-abiding and positive behaviour in and out of school
- Develop positive relationships and choose not to bully and discriminate
- Develop self-confidence and successfully deal with significant life changes and challenges
- Develop enterprising behaviour
- Parents, carers and families promote positive behaviour

(DfES, 2004d: 5)

Here too we see the emphasis on responsibility, engagement and trust. The case for 'education for community' is recognised by Smith (2001) as a strong one and can be found in the works of Dewey, Putnam and Buber. However, there are inevitable tensions in the teaching of citizenship. There are questions about whose community and whose values pervade.

At what point are children or young people considered to be active citizens and allowed to take a stand on the issues that concern them? Pupil protests over the Iraq war were an interesting case. Citizenship education can be seen more realistically as preparing citizens-in-waiting for an active role in the future. It is about raising political awareness and developing political literacy, whilst at the same time seeking to establish the skills necessary for community engagement. Emphasis is on behaviour management both in and out of school. Those who fail to engage in law-abiding, positive behaviours threaten social cohesion and must be targeted through corrective education and the law, hence the New Labour government's *Respect* agenda and the imposition of anti-social behaviour orders (ASBOs).

Making sense of community

The term 'community' can mask a number of different meanings and interpretations. It can relate to geographical areas, physical neighbourhoods or groups of people linked by common interest: religious, economic, cultural or ethnic. In political discourse 'community' can be used as a powerful organising tool. It defines who is 'included' and who is 'excluded' as well as highlighting collective values and perceived threats. Smith (2001) uses 'place' (locality), 'interest' (non-place forms of community, e.g. academic, religious, ethnic or cyber) and 'communion' (a spirit of community) to explore the meanings of 'community'. There is of course a degree of overlap between these. Smith (2001) also cites Lee and Newby (1983) in understanding community in terms of social networks. The fact that people live next to one another does not necessarily mean that they have much to do with one another. It is the social networks that they create with family and friends that count. This resonates with Putnam's discourse of 'social capital'.

> For a variety of reasons, life is easier in a community blessed with a substantial stock of social capital. In the first place, networks of civic engagement foster sturdy norms of generalized reciprocity and encourage the emergence of social trust. Such networks facilitate coordination and communication, amplify reputations, and thus allow dilemmas of collective action to be resolved. When economic and political negotiation is embedded in dense networks of social interaction, incentives for opportunism are reduced. At the same time, networks of civic engagement embody past success at collaboration, which can serve as a cultural template for future collaboration. Finally,

> dense networks of interaction probably broaden the participants' sense of self, developing the "I" into the "we," or (in the language of rational-choice theorists) enhancing the participants' "taste" for collective benefits.
>
> (Putnam, 1995: 66)

Community regeneration and development

Underpinning *ECM* is a concern about the negative effects on children of growing up in poor or disaffected communities and the generational cycle of deprivation and exclusion. Community regeneration was an explicit policy focus for New Labour, a means of encouraging social cohesion, and was linked closely to the notion of 'active citizenship'. It is an example of targeted government policy. The government body responsible for such programmes was the Office of the Deputy Prime Minister (ODPM), later to be replaced by the Department for Communities and Local Government (DCLG).

The first report from the Social Exclusion Unit was entitled *Bringing Britain Together: a National Strategy for Neighbourhood Renewal* (SEU, 1998) and advocated the involvement of communities in regeneration programmes. Between 1999 and 2000 eighteen Policy Action Teams were set up under the remit of the SEU to examine detailed aspects of social exclusion. In 2001 the National Strategy for Neighbourhood Renewal was launched, taking a holistic approach to the problems of degeneration. An interim report, *Making it Happen in Neighbourhoods: The National Strategy for Neighbourhood Renewal,* was published in 2005 (SEU, 2005). Central to its argument was the focus on putting local communities at the heart of the decision-making process, drawing on the strengths of the public, private and voluntary sector (Kettle, 2008: 186). At the same time, the Academy for Sustainable Communities was launched following the recommendations of the Egan Review to 'lead on and provide focus for continuous skills development among all occupations engaged in delivering sustainable communities' (ODPM, 2004: 80).

This links with understandings of community empowerment:

> the process of enabling people to shape and choose the services they use on a personal basis, so that they can influence the way those services are delivered.
>
> (Communities and Local Government, 2009)

In adopting a more holistic approach to community regeneration, New Labour focused on specific areas of degeneration and disadvantage. These became the focus for the first *Sure Start* centres and the Excellence in Cities initiative, later to become Education Action Zones (EAZs). The Academies programme also targeted those deprived areas and 'failing schools' in an attempt to tackle underachievement and disadvantage. Continuing the theme of public–private collaboration and partnership, together with the standards agenda, academies were seen as a way of bringing much-needed investment into state education, particularly in relation to underachieving schools in deprived areas. In theory at least they offered the potential of greater community collaboration in the creation of new schools more responsive to local needs.

A less controversial feature of *ECM* was the development of the extended schools initiative. This again had at its centre the desire to position schools at the heart of the community and had its roots in the UK in the work of the SEU. The extended school offer provided supervision for children between 8am and 6pm throughout the year, to facilitate families into work and to encourage local participation. The core offer for mainstream and special schools was:

- high quality 'wrap-around' childcare provided on the school site or through other local providers, with supervised transfer arrangements where appropriate, available 8am–6pm all year round;
- a varied menu of activities to be on offer such as homework clubs and study support, sport (at least two hours a week beyond the school day for those who want it), music tuition, dance and drama, arts and crafts, special interest clubs such as chess and first aid courses, visits to museums and galleries, learning a foreign language, volunteering, business and enterprise activities;
- parenting support including information sessions for parents at key transition points, parenting programmes run with the support of other children's services and family learning sessions to allow children to learn with their parents;
- swift and easy referral to a wide range of specialist support services such as speech therapy, child and adolescent mental health services, family support services, intensive behaviour support, and (for young people) sexual health services. Some may be delivered on school sites;
- providing wider community access to ICT, sports and arts facilities, including adult learning.

(DfES, 2005a: 8)

Schools were to work closely with parents to shape these activities around the needs of their community and were to choose to provide extra services in response to parental demand. The core offer ensured that all children and parents had access to a minimum of services and activities (DfES, 2006b). By 2010 all schools were expected to provide the full core offer, either individually or in confederation with neighbouring schools.

Conclusion

Under New Labour, promoting active citizenship met a number of government aims. It increased an individual's stake in society and raised the potential of local people influencing the services that they used. This in turn aimed to promote a sense of ownership of government reforms. It provided a means of developing skills and knowledge amongst the population that would enhance community cohesion and participation. Finally, it was a means of furthering the government's modernisation agenda via new public management. However, there were inevitable tensions within such a far-reaching policy objective. Defining who or what is community is not clear cut, and sets up barriers between those considered part of the 'community 'and those outside. It raises issues concerning values and who determines what is acceptable and what is not. Furthermore, pursuing the choice agenda has militated against community cohesion. Parents can educate their children outside the local neighbourhood where the interaction between friends, family and neighbours have been shown to be fundamental to civic society. *ECM*, however, has raised awareness of the negative effects for children and families of living in deprived neighbourhoods and has provided a much-needed vehicle for targeted intervention and redistribution of resources. The question remains as to how far such intervention amounts to an effective participatory role in civil society, empowerment and social cohesion or is effectively social control and compliance.

Chapter 9

Challenging parents

Government *in loco parentis*

Introduction

Every Child Matters (DfES, 2003a) endorsed New Labour's notion of a 'new relationship' with parents. Parents were given a central role in promoting and achieving the five outcomes for children, ensuring that their own children remained safe and healthy, and that they could enjoy and achieve, make a positive contribution and attain economic wellbeing. This chapter highlights the positioning of parents as agents of government policy and the tensions for parents that *ECM* presented. Any failure of children to take advantage of the educational, social and economic opportunities available to them rested with parents rather than government or service providers. The chapter explores the notions of 'parental responsibility', 'parental involvement' and the concept of the 'good parent' that New Labour sought to model through *Every Child Matters.*

Understanding parents

Parents have long been acknowledged as the child's first educator and they have a number of responsibilities in law. 'Parental responsibility' as a legal term was introduced in Section 2 of the Children Act 1989 and is defined as 'all rights, duties, powers, responsibilities and authority that go with being a parent' (Walker, 2008b: 25). Although the law does not define in detail the notion of parental responsibility, government does set out the key roles of parents. These include:

- providing a home for the child;
- having contact with and living with the child;
- protecting and maintaining the child;
- disciplining the child;
- choosing and providing for the child's education;
- determining the religion of the child;

- agreeing to the child's medical treatment;
- naming the child and agreeing to any change of the child's name;
- accompanying the child outside the UK and agreeing to the child's emigration, should the issue arise;
- being responsible for the child's property;
- appointing a guardian for the child, if necessary;
- allowing confidential information about the child being disclosed.

(Directgov, 2009)

However, not all parents are vested with parental responsibility. According to law in England and Wales, all mothers are, but it is not the case for all fathers. A father only has legal responsibility if he is married to the mother at the time of the birth, or if he and the mother have jointly adopted the child. Fathers can obtain parental responsibility by jointly registering the birth of the child with the mother, by forming a parental responsibility agreement with the mother or by way of a parental responsibility order made by a court (ibid.). According to Walker (2008b: 25) 'parents who have it never lose parental responsibility, even if their children are taken into care and made subject of a Care Order'. In a society where statistically more than one in three children are born outside marriage, this inevitably means that the weight of parental responsibility lies with the mother. Carers can be siblings, other family members, neighbours or statutory and voluntary carers such as foster carers and residential care staff (Leverett, 2008: 48). It is important to note, therefore, that those who have parental responsibility for children may not necessarily be those engaged in parenting. According to the DfES (2006b: 3) parents include 'mothers, fathers, carers and other adults with responsibility for caring for a child, including looked-after children'. This is significant when considering to whom policy initiatives such as *Every Child Matters* are directed.

The concept of parental responsibility encapsulated in the 1989 Children Act in no way threatened the traditional *laissez-faire* parent/state relationship. Parenting continued to be viewed as a private enterprise not subject to state intervention unless children were identified as being 'at risk'. However, the Conservative government's neo-liberal notion of partnership (which was advanced throughout the 1980s and 1990s) and the business model of target setting and accountability, was adopted as the way forward for state governance. This followed a model of citizen rights in which the public had the right to expect certain standards and performance from state-run organisations. It was demonstrated to improve public services in the inauguration of the Citizens' Charter in 1991.

Patients of the National Health Service were offered a Patients' Charter and parents were provided with a Parents' Charter. The Citizens' Charter and its derivatives opened up the public sector to increased scrutiny and control whilst allowing a greater centralisation of power for government in setting priorities and targets (Clarke and Newman, 1997: 110). New Labour continued the neo-liberal trend begun by the Conservatives, but added a stronger level of state intervention. According to Leverett (2008: 51), since 1997 the state became more willing to intervene with a range of specific social and economic policy initiatives related to anti-social behaviour, poverty, educational standards, and revitalising the labour market. These initiatives directly involved or affected parents. Partnership with parents became part of government rhetoric. This led to an increase in state levels of support for, and surveillance of, parents (Leverett, 2008). In practice the strategy was to identify specific groups of parents according to gender, social class, ethnicity, culture and economic identities. It was these groups of parents, rather than parents *per se*, who were repositioned in relation to state intervention and policy making.

Understanding partnership

The concept of partnership is both ill-defined and complex. It is closely linked to notions of involvement, participation, power and accountability. Ball (2008: 142) argues that the meaning of partnership in relation to practice is often 'vague and slippery and carries dangers of being made meaningless by overuse'. Furthermore, he argues that in New Labour discourse it dissolves important differences between the public, private and voluntary sector modes of working and 'obscures the role of financial relationships and power imbalances between partners' (ibid.). In this way partnerships play a significant role in the construction of new public management systems of governance. Partnership assumes understandings of citizenship and active involvement on both a local and a national scale. It is (in theory at least) about government working *with* society rather than directing it from above (Teisman and Klijn, 2002).

Hudson and Hardy (2002: 51) link New Labour's adoption of 'partnership' and 'joined up government' with a willingness to embrace complexity theory in relation to the sphere of public service interests. Public services are there to combat 'wicked issues': those problems spanning organisational and professional boundaries. Partnership and collaboration also mark the government's rejection of competition inherent in the open market (ibid.).

The rhetoric of partnership applies to both vertical and horizontal partnerships. And herein lies the tension. Using lessons learned from the expansion of the Rotterdam harbour, Teisman and Klijn (2002) investigate the substantive nature of partnership in the outworking of government policy. Their observations suggest that in reality 'partnership' equates to little more than 'contracting out' rather than joint decision making and continuity. In other words government notions of partnership do not necessarily result in any immediate change from traditional unilateral decision-making processes. The public sector was still based on hierarchical demand mechanisms, controlled by top administrators and politicians. It is within this hierarchy that government retains its superior position. Politicians impose their demands on society, rather than society imposing their demands on politicians. Thus, although governments have adopted the rhetoric of partnership and cooperation, in reality they are dedicated to their own procedures, rules and principles of control. In this way partnerships are more likely to be made to fit into traditional policy-making procedures and resemble contracted-out schemes rather than being based upon understandings of equity, collaboration and trust.

There are several extant models of partnership, especially in relation to education and social care. Hudson and Hardy (2002) identify six key principles of partnership:

1 Acknowledging the need of partnership. It is a prerequisite that partners have an appreciation of their interdependencies.
2 Clarity and realism of purpose. Partnership should be based on an explicit statement of shared vision, underpinned by jointly held values.
3 Commitment and ownership. This has to do with 'leadership, ownership, entrepreneurship and institutionalisation' and is dependent upon individual commitment to the venture at the most senior levels.
4 The development and maintenance of trust. The more trust there is, the better the chances for successful partnership. Partnerships work best where each partner is perceived to have equivalent status.
5 The establishment of clear and robust partnership arrangements. This has to do with rules of engagement. Arrangements for partnership working should be as unambiguous and straightforward as possible. A main requirement is that the partnership's focus should be on the processes and outcomes of those partnerships, rather than the inputs and structures.

6 Monitoring and review of organisational learning. This relates to both reflective and reflexive elements of partnership working. Monitoring, reviewing and learning is an essential way of assessing performance and the process by which commitment and trust are cemented.

The model of partnership evident through *ECM*, however, looks very different from the above and resembles far more closely the contracted-out arrangement described by Teisman and Klijn (2002). Furthermore, these principles closely resemble those outlined by the Conservative government (DH, 1996) for full partnership. Significantly this document recognises four successive levels of partnership:

- **Level 1** providing information
- **Level 2** involvement
- **Level 3** participation
- **Level 4** full partnership.

ECM restricted parents to the first two rungs of this ladder by concentrating on providing parents with information and encouraging access to and involvement with services.

Partnership between parents and the state

Every Child Matters is significant in terms of the degree to which New Labour publically set out their expectations of parents. Parents were to be actively engaged in supporting their children to achieve the five outcomes. In this way *ECM* was directed not only to all parents vested with parental responsibility, but also to those who engaged in parenting roles without such legal accountability.

Parents' and carers' roles are clearly stated in *Every Child Matters: Change for Children in Schools* (DfES, 2004d), as Table 9.1 shows.

In order for parents to succeed in these obligations, *Every Child Matters* (DfES, 2003a) proposed a range of support mechanisms for parents:

- Universal services such as schools, health and social services providing information and advice and engaging parents to support their child's development, where such support is needed or wanted.
- Targeted specialist support to parents of children requiring additional support.

Table 9.1 EMC outcomes and the role of parents

ECM outcomes	*Role of parents*
Be healthy	
Physically healthy	
Mentally and emotionally healthy	
Sexually healthy	
Healthy lifestyles	
Choose not to take illegal drugs	Parents, carers and families promote healthy choices
Stay safe	
Safe from maltreatment, neglect, violence and sexual exploitation	
Safe from accidental injury and death	
Safe from bullying and discrimination	
Safe from crime and anti-social behaviour in and out of school	
Have security, stability and are cared for	Parents, carers and families provide safe homes and stability
Enjoy and achieve	
Ready for school	
Attend and enjoy school	
Achieve stretching national educational standards at primary school	
Achieve personal and social development and enjoy recreation	
Achieve stretching national educational standards at secondary school	Parents, carers and families support learning
Make a positive contribution	
Engage in decision-making and support the community and environment	
Engage in law-abiding and positive behaviour in and out of school	
Develop positive relationships and choose not to bully and discriminate	
Develop self-confidence and successfully deal with significant life changes and challenges	
Develop enterprising behaviour	Parents, carers and families promote positive behaviour
Achieve economic wellbeing	
Engage in further education, employment or training on leaving school	
Ready for employment	
Live in decent homes and sustainable communities	
Access to transport and material goods	
Live in households free from low income	Parents, carers and families are supported to be economically active

(Adapted from DfES, 2004d: 5)

- Compulsory action through Parenting Orders as a last resort where parents are condoning a child's anti-social behaviour such as truancy or offending.

(DfES, 2003a: 39)

Suggestions for universal parenting services included a national helpline, parent information meetings at key transition points, family learning programmes, support programmes for fathers as well as mothers, improved communication between parents and schools with childcare, early years education social care and schools working more closely with parents modelling the *Sure Start* children's centres, and joint training on development and behaviour issues for professionals (DfES, 2003a). To this end, government promoted support via multi-agency services, parenting support guidance for local authorities (LAs) and placed a statutory requirement on LAs to provide information, advice and assistance to parents from April 2008. Professionals were supported by the National Academy for Parenting Practitioners announced in 2007 (Parenting Academy, 2007). The Common Assessment Framework (CAF) allowed professionals across children's services to assess parenting capacity: the ability of parents or carers to provide basic care, ensure safety and protection and to provide emotional warmth, stability, guidance, boundaries and stimulation for their children (CWDC, 2007). In addition extended schools or children's centres offered on-site childcare from 8am to 6pm which was intended both to facilitate the transition and sustainability of getting previously unemployed parents and carers into work and to allow for 'swift and easy referral to a wide range of specialist support services' (DfES, 2005a: 8).

The concept of human and social capital was explained in Chapter 1. Governments are interested in investing in human capital to create the skilled and educated workforce which is essential to a competitive economic nation state. Parents invest in their children's human capital via the education system, and their ability to do so is linked to their own measure of human capital. Social capital is about individual capacity operating via networks (family, friends, associates) and within communities (services and agencies) to pursue personal goals. It is the means by which parents are able to develop their children's human capacity. Intervention programmes such as *Sure Start* and *ECM* were intended to develop social capital and the transference of accepted norms of behaviour or responsibility among communities for the common good. However, if social capital can be described as parents knowing *who* can help in achieving their goals for their children, cultural capital is about knowing *how* to do this (Leverett, 2008: 62). Middle-class parents vested with high levels of cultural capital are more likely to be successful in exercising parental choice: selecting a school for their child, gaining access for them to higher education and thus professional employment. This is particularly so for parents with economic capital – the physical and material resources necessary to realise aspirations. In a capitalist society, economic capital can be exchanged for products and services (Leverett, 2008: 58). This follows the individualism of neo-liberalism. New Labour social policy was about raising the economic capacity of the most deprived and breaking the cycle of deprivation in which their children can become trapped. The acquisition of one type of capital can be used as investment to obtain others. New Labour's positioning of targeted groups of parents was about achieving this end. Yet it was the individual, rather than parent groups collectively, who must engage with this.

Partnership between parents and schools/professionals/practitioners

At various times in history parents have either been seen as the unwanted guest on school premises or the welcome ally. The Plowden Report (CACE, 1967), referred to in Chapter 10, advocated parental partnership with schools, stressing that it was a school's duty to encourage parental interest in their children's learning and that levels of achievement would thereby improve. However, according to Vincent (1996) the aim was to

> convert as many *individual* parents as possible to supporting the goals of the school ... Plowden embodied a consensus view of home–school relationships, stretching the school's walls to include those parents who were cooperative and supportive.
>
> Vincent (1996: 25)

New Labour under the *ECM* agenda took on the duty of encouraging parents to engage in partnership with schools (and schools with parents) and to supply the necessary supports for those with limited resources to do so. The government promoted parents' partnership with schools on the basis of added benefits for both children and parents. These were listed as follows.

For Children

- accelerated development of oracy and pre-literacy skills
- improved standards in numeracy and literacy
- positive behavioural and attitudinal changes
- enhanced confidence and self-esteem
- awareness that learning is a normal activity throughout life
- pleasure from collaborative learning.

For Parents

- improved competence in literacy and numeracy
- progression for over 50 per cent of participants to FE and training or more challenging jobs
- increased confidence in contacts with schools, teachers, and the education system leading to becoming more active partners with schools
- a greater understanding of child development and of the strategies that can be used to help children to learn at key points in development
- improved parenting
- better relationships with children.

(DfES, 2003b: 4)

Such aims stand clearly within the intended outcomes of the *ECM* agenda, enhancing individual human and social capital. Partnership with schools involves:

- supporting the five outcomes (see Table 9.1);
- supporting the child's learning – reading at home, helping with homework, attending parent/teacher meetings, parent mentors;
- supporting the school – providing help in the classroom, parent–teacher associations (PTA), governorship, helping at extended school services such as breakfast clubs and after-school clubs.

Vincent (1996: 44) defines parents' roles in state education as:

- supporter/learner – to support professionals and adopt their concerns and approaches;
- consumer – to encourage school accountability and high standards (via league tables and parental choice);
- participant – to be involved in governance of the school as well as education of their own child.

The list presupposes a degree of social, economic, cultural and human capital on the part of parents. Those without such capacity because of socio-economic status, ethnicity, language, gender or political status (economic or political migrants, refugees) are most likely to be included in the 'hard to reach' category thus diminishing further their capacity to invest in their children's futures.

One way of providing interventionist support and making services more accessible was through extended schools (see Chapter 11) or children's centres which brought together a range of professionals in one place to serve the needs of targeted groups. This model of multi-agency working was one of the fundamental principles underpinning *ECM* and was intended to facilitate parental/family partnership with services and to produce more effective, targeted provision. Extended schools offered non-working or unemployed parents a route into the world of work by providing basic education and training or family learning to achieve qualifications and to improve skills. Moreover, they offered childcare from 8am to 6pm for the working parent.

Conclusion

New Labour education and social policy on parents was determined by the desire for social inclusion, raising educational standards and the eradication of child poverty, represented by a social intergrationist discourse. The boundary between inclusion/exclusion was made explicit, namely the world of paid employment (Darling, 1997: 10). Investment in education, training and skills was to move from exclusion to inclusion: from the outside to the inside. This was intended to accumulate human, social, cultural and economic capital. It was also about redistribution and tackling poverty by creating a more equitable society, with the state ensuring educational and training opportunities rather than guaranteed outcomes. Those groups of parents trapped within, or at risk of, deprivation formed the focus of such policy initiatives.

Targeting those sections of the population (including parents) that threatened social cohesion, and were vulnerable to social exclusion, allowed for immediate needs in society to be addressed. For some groups particularly, this legitimised state intervention into the very heart of family life – parenting. The Family and Parenting Institute (2008) list 139 policies relating to parents in the years 1997–2008, the majority since 2005, including *Every Parent Matters* (DfES, 2007b).

However, identifying and tackling the obstacles to social inclusion simultaneously created the conditions for social exclusion: in the discourse about parenting, identifying standards for 'good parenting' highlighted the behaviours and attitudes associated with 'poor' parenting. Policy formulation in relation to parents became a matter of:

- mobilising middle-class parents in the exercise of school choice or through active participation, e.g. as members of governing bodies;
- supporting and training working-class parents through better access to services, parenting classes, education and training; and
- monitoring parents through surveillance and control by way of parenting orders and actions against absentee fathers.

Of course, the policy was well intentioned. But an underlying deficit model is inescapable: working-class children need the government *in loco parentis*.

Chapter 10

Multi-agency working

Plowden revisited

Introduction

The chosen mechanism for achieving the aims of *ECM* – multi-agency working – was neither new nor innovative. The Plowden Report (CACE, 1967) made recommendations for professional partnership between schools and social workers to improve their effectiveness for the child. It was a central tenet of child-centred education. The same model for the delivery of frontline services of education, health and social services forty years later, in the era of child-centred social policy, comes as no surprise. *ECM* promoted the notion of multi-agency working, but provided no models of practice. It was for local authorities and agencies to work it out for themselves. How successful multi-agency approaches have worked in practice, what might be the barriers to inter-professional working and training, and whether this is indeed the best model for the most serious and complex cases, are discussed in this chapter. The strategy coincided with enormous changes at local authority and government department level under the guise of new public management (NPM) (see Chapter 2). We look at the ways in which local authorities planned for and provided multi-agency responses to child welfare issues in a context of change and innovation.

The rationale for multi-agency working

Every Child Matters (DfES, 2003a) and guidance documents such as *Working Together to Safeguard Children* (DfES, 2006c), took a positive, proactive approach to safeguarding children and promoting their welfare in an attempt to reduce the need for intervention by state agencies. Promoting welfare widened the responsibility for tackling social exclusion beyond the traditional remit of universal services such as health and education. It included numerous agencies across the private, public and voluntary sectors. The whole workforce based around children, young people and families, was to operate together to provide joined-up, multi-agency responses to the complex issues of safeguarding children.

Since 1997, government attention has focused on constructing social policy around child welfare. Reports such as the Laming Inquiry (HMSO, 2003) contributed to a shift away from diagnostic approaches, symptomatic of traditional child protection measures, to more proactive, holistic methodologies based on understandings of wellbeing. The publication of *Every Child Matters* (DfES, 2003a) and *The Children Act* (HMSO, 2004) continued not only government's restructuring of the public sector via new public management, but also its child-focused reforms. These were aimed at reducing the negative impacts of those wider forces implicit in society deemed to limit the life chances and opportunities of the most vulnerable. The approach resonates with Bronfenbrenner's (1979) Ecological Systems Theory; it addressed the need to understand the world around the child and the way various environmental layers help or hinder development (Adams and Tucker, 2007).

Implicit in the documents is an understanding of the complex needs of the most vulnerable children, young people and families in modern-day society. The underlying assumption is that inter-related problems such as health, social housing, finance and education can be dealt with by adopting inter-related or multi-agency approaches to service delivery. The expectation is that all agencies to do with child welfare – private, public and voluntary – will work together to achieve the five *ECM* outcomes: to stay safe, healthy, enjoy and achieve, promote economic wellbeing and to make a positive contribution (DfES, 2004d). Rustin (2004) suggests that the Laming Report presented a series of recommendations that focused on the institutional and personal failings of the key agencies and personnel involved in the Climbié case. It served merely to replicate the deficiencies of the dominant style of public service management, one focused on objectives and targets. A judgement based on 'processes' and 'outputs' in turn produced a 'processes' and 'outputs' solution. *Every Child Matters* (DfES, 2003a) and the subsequent *Children's Plan* (DCSF, 2007b) concentrated on such priorities as 'information sharing', 'multi-agency working', 'joined-up support', 'co-operative working practices' and the 'co-location of services' in order to prevent vulnerable children and families 'falling through the net'. The proposed Children's Workforce Action Plan had a remit of strengthening 'integrated working across all services' (DCSF, 2007b).

Government proposals for more integrated working led to the notion of an integrated Children's Workforce that was to be managed at a strategic level in each Local Authority by the formation of Children's Trusts. Publications such as *Building a World-Class Workforce for Children and Young People and their Families* (DfES, 2006d) and *Building an Integrated Qualifications Framework* (DfES, 2006e) highlighted the key issues to be addressed. There was an acknowledgement that the climate in which the children's workforce operated was in a state of flux because of the restructuring of welfare services and the consequent blurring of sector boundaries. Citing findings from the *Effective Provision of Pre-school Education* (EPPE) project (Sylva *et al.*, 2004), the government seemed committed to the belief that a 'flexible, skilled and motivated workforce' is a major factor in the provision of better services (DfES, 2006b: 3). Reducing the complexity of qualifications and assessment would allow for 'greater flexibility and movement between work in different kinds of settings and service' (DfES, 2006b: 3). The Integrated Qualifications Framework is a set of approved qualifications that allowed for progression, continuing professional development and mobility across the children and young people's workforce. It was drawn up on the belief that there was a 'common core of skills and knowledge' that could be drawn upon across the wide range of agencies involved in supporting children's welfare. These were set out in the 2005 document of that name:

- effective communication and engagement
- child and young person development
- safeguarding and promoting the welfare of the child
- supporting transitions
- multi-agency working
- sharing information.

(DfES, 2005b)

The benefits of multi-agency working and the development of integrated services belonged to both service providers and service users.

Approaches to multi-agency working

The call for inter-agency working and greater collaboration between schools and social services in the *Every Child Matters* agenda originated in the Plowden Report on primary education as long ago as 1967:

> We think the following arguments carry great weight: (a) workers in a variety of services are increasingly finding they are concerned with similar families having similar needs; (b) the atomisation of social

> services leads to contradictory policies and to situations in which 'everybody's business becomes nobody's business'; (c) continuity of care is difficult under present arrangements; (d) a more unified structure would provide better opportunities for appraising needs and planning how to meet them; (e) it would also accord with the present tendency of social work to treat people as members of families and local groups rather than to deal with specific individuals or separate needs isolated from their social context; (f) it would make it possible to create viable teams to operate in areas of special need. Although such teams should cover carefully selected areas they could be physically located in many different places, for instance in clinics, in the local offices of welfare and children's departments, or medical group practices. Since all children spend several hours a day in school for most of the year, and since it is relatively easy for parents to visit schools, there is much to be said for choosing the schools as a base for social work units responsible for helping families facing many kinds of difficulties.
>
> (CACE, 1967, para. 240)

The model of multi-agency working recommended here is just one of several in the literature. One taxonomy by Atkinson *et al.* (2002) of multi-agency working across education, social services and health, identifies five models of practice:

- Decision-making groups – a forum, generally at strategic level, where professionals from different agencies come together to discuss ideas and make decisions.
- Consultation and training – generally at operational level, professionals from one agency provide consultation or training to enhance the expertise of those of another.
- Centre-based delivery – at operational level this model represents the gathering a range of expertise in one place in order to deliver a more coordinated and comprehensive service.
- Coordinated delivery – similar to centre-based delivery this model, again at the operational level, is enhanced by the appointment of a coordinator responsible for drawing together previously disparate services.
- Operational team delivery – again at the operational level, professionals from different agencies work together on a day to day basis to form a cohesive team that deliver services directly to clients.

(Atkinson *et al.*, 2002)

The study concluded that decision-making groups and coordinated delivery were the most common amongst their sample. Earlier models identified in the Audit Commission Report of 1998, and cited by Atkinson *et al.* (2002: 4), include the formation of:

- a new and separate legal entity – where agencies come together to form a new organisation with an identity separate from any of the partners;
- a virtual organisation – where a separate organisation is formed without the need of generating a new legal identity;
- co-locating of staff from partner organisations;
- steering groups without dedicated resources.

Despite this, no specific models of multi-agency working were explicitly recommended in the legislative documents. Multi-agency working met the government's modernisation agenda for welfare services as well as being the preferred means of service delivery for clients. The *Every Child Matters* website lists three models under the category of integrated working which equate to the Atkinson *et al.* (2002) taxonomy:

- Multi agency panels – professionals employed by their home agencies meet together on a regular basis for the purposes of assessment and information sharing i.e. operating at strategic level. Panels could be coordinated by a panel manager. Other titles may include 'network', 'panel' or 'team around the child'.
- Multi agency teams – A more formal arrangement than a panel. Practitioners are seconded or recruited into a team and generally share a base. They were to work with universal services at operational level.
- Integrated services – These equate to coordinated/ operational team delivery under the Atkinson *et al.* definition and acted as a 'service hub' for the community. Generally working out of a school or early years setting, professionals were to work together and were more likely to experience joint training and joint working, perhaps in smaller multi agency teams. *SureStart* centres would be the exemplar here.

(CWDC, 2007)

The reorganisation in June 2007 of the DfES into the Department for Children Schools and Families (DCSF) and the Department for Universities, Innovation and Skills (DIUS) (from 2009, Business,

Innovation and Skills) indicated the government's continued commitment to coordinated working at the highest level. However, any notion that chosen models of multi-agency working were fixed, either at strategic level or at point of delivery, would be to simplify the complex, and far from coherently-structured, approaches by local authorities and primary care trusts. Under the practices of new public management, sector boundaries were becoming less distinct, limiting the traditional hold by professionals and thereby facilitating the adoption of government policy at local and operational levels. These initiatives challenged the traditional contours of the public service sector and professional practice.

Barriers to multi-agency working

According to Frost and Parton (2009: 46), the call for the integration of children's services 'required the personalisation and integration of universal services which would also provide easy access to effective and targeted specialist services'. This meant that childcare, early-years services, schools and health services would be integrated into new arrangements. Such arrangements included the melding of public, private and voluntary sector organisations, agencies and funding. It led to the imperative for common processes to be adopted across agencies such as the Common Assessment Framework (CAF), a common language of communication between agencies and for use with clients, and more effective information sharing via the Information Sharing Index (ISI). There were inevitably to be tensions within both policy-making and practice arising from such an agenda.

The use of new forms of information and communication technology underpinned New Labour's drive to modernise government and public services. E-government or 'transformational government' is about 'improving internal managerial efficiency and the quality of public services to citizens' (Moon, 2002: 424). However, there were deep-seated concerns over the e-government agenda, particularly in relation to data protection issues and privacy. Under Section 12 of the Children Act 2004, local authorities were expected to operate a national information sharing index intended to facilitate the *ECM* five outcomes and 'improving the wellbeing of *all* children' (Frost and Parton, 2009: 50). It was not intended to focus primarily on child protection issues. However, there were serious reservations concerning the cost of implementing such a system, the ethical considerations of information sharing and the responses of young people to the breach of their privacy (Frost and Parton, 2009).

The Foundation for Information Policy Research report of 2006 (Anderson *et al.*, 2006: 1) highlighted the tensions in the distinctions between child protection measures and child wellbeing, and between measures intended for the protection of the child and those for the protection of the community. The report raised questions about 'e-discrimination', 'the scarcity of effective intervention programmes', the interpretation of data protection and privacy laws, and the potential harm that information sharing might cause.

In response to such concerns the national information sharing index evolved into a less ambitious ContactPoint, which went live in May 2009:

> ContactPoint will provide a quick way for authorised practitioners to find out who else is working with the same child or young person. It will support better communication among practitioners across education, health, social care and youth offending, in the statutory and voluntary sectors. It's a simple online tool which holds:
>
> - minimal identifying information for each child in England: name, address, date of birth, gender, and contact details for parents or carers. Each child also has a unique identifying number;
> - contact details for the child's educational setting and GP practice and for other practitioners or services working with the child; and
> - an indication as to whether a service or practitioner holds an assessment under the Common Assessment Framework, or whether they are a lead professional for that child.
>
> (DCSF, 2009d)

Atkinson *et al.* (2002) cite seven key challenges to multi-agency working, of which communication was one:

- fiscal resources
- roles and responsibilities
- competing priorities
- non-fiscal resources (time, staff, pace)
- communication
- professional and agency cultures
- management.

These issues reappear in the 2009 Laming Report following the death of 'Baby P' and in the Children's Workforce Development Council (CWDC) evaluation report for 2007/8 (CWDC, 2009). Laming also identified knowledge, skills and the need for high-quality training as fundamental to the effective delivery of multi-agency/integrated working.

One model of this can be found in the training of health and allied-health professionals. The government rationale for common training was an acknowledgement that the climate within which the Children's Workforce was operating was in a state of flux, partly because of the stepped *Every Child Matters* reform agenda and the consequent blurring of sector boundaries, but also because of financial imperatives and the changing workforce. The government seemed committed to the belief that a 'flexible, skilled and motivated workforce was a major factor in the provision of better services' (DfES, 2006b: 3). The history of Inter-Professional Learning (IPL) in Health and Social care in the UK can be traced as far back as the 1960s and has since developed in response to a range of differing agendas. What is significant, however, is the lack of policy attention paid to Inter-Professional Education (IPE) in other areas. The Social Care Institute of Excellence (SCIE) identified this as a striking 'gap in relation to preparing professionals in children's services' (Sharland *et al.*, 2007). Whereas health professionals such as nurses, hospital social workers and pediatricians may expect to experience joint training by equally diverse training professionals, it is not the normal experience of trainee teachers either during their initial training or in subsequent years of practice. The potential benefits for effective multi-agency practice of teachers learning alongside social workers, educational psychologists or speech therapists should not be ignored. This has formed the basis of a number of recent research studies such as the ESRC-funded *Learning in and for Multi-agency Working Project* (Daniels *et al.*, 2007), and research into the development of Continuing Professional Development (CPD) courses across the Children's Workforce (Coombs and Simon, forthcoming). One of the major barriers appears to be the complexity of funding arrangements for professional development courses. In the absence of a central funding body, professional bodies, local authorities and primary care trusts have yet to work together more effectively in the development of multi- or inter-professional training programmes. The example of IPL would indicate that opportunities for joint professional training should also be embedded within undergraduate professional courses. Furthermore, whilst the development of multi-agency working linked to education is still in relative infancy, the expertise of potential trainers/educators for such practices is also limited.

Conclusion

Whether a multi-agency approach is necessarily the best method of tackling the most serious of child welfare cases is still open to debate. The success of any model of 'best practice' is situated within professional culture and social context. There should be natural reservations about promoting 'best practice' models in the assumption that one size fits all. There is still an emphasis on target-setting and inspection regimes as a tool for improvement evidenced in the 2009 Laming Report, but organisational tools that focus on systems and outputs may well miss the plight of the child or family at the centre. Frontline services are at their most stretched in the most deprived areas, and suffer from low recruitment, heavy caseloads and poor retention, which in turn become part of the problem. Measures for ensuring child safeguarding and wellbeing must not be divorced from those tackling the root causes of neglect and abuse, namely social inequality expressed through poor housing, unemployment and poverty.

Chapter 11

Redefining the education sector

The challenge for schools

Introduction

In the wider political context of New Labour's neo-liberal Third Way politics, it is not just frontline services such as health and social services, which are adopting new models of working. By constructing welfare policy around the child, the government attempted to redefine the very nature of the education service. There is a fundamental shift in the key responsibilities and remit of education. Whereas traditionally education held a core responsibility for only one aspect of all children's lives, namely teaching and learning, it was given much broader and holistic responsibility for *all aspects* of the lives of the most vulnerable children. This was underlined by the changes to the Department for Education and Skills (DfES) which was divided into two strategic departments, one for Children, Schools and Families (DCSF), the other for Innovation, Universities and Skills (DIUS, later Business, Innovation and Skills, BIS). It was the new DCSF that was to lead in creating coherence for children, schools and families across Whitehall. Significantly, the title of 'Education' has been lost from these departments. This points to the constructing of a wider, more complex and all-encompassing education sector in which schools, rather than traditional understandings of 'education' were to play a significant yet different role.

The changing role of schools

ECM calls for an holistic approach both to the way in which children and young people are viewed and understood and in the delivery of services to them. In this way *ECM* challenges traditional understandings about the nature of education and raises questions about what concept of 'education' can support such a wide-ranging and holistic approach. One response has been to define 'education-in-its-broadest-sense' (EBS) which Moss and Haydon (2008) describe as

> a broad concept that understands education as fostering and supporting the general well-being of children and young people, and their ability to interact effectively with their environment and to live a good life. This is education as a process of upbringing and increasing participation in the wider society.
>
> (Moss and Haydon, 2008: 2)

Such a concept has resonance with early years and primary education and there are similarities with the wider European notion of social pedagogy (*Sozial Pädagogik*) with its roots in nineteenth-century German progressive education. Social pedagogy links social work and education in such a way as to be sometimes termed 'community education' or 'education for sociality' (Smith, 2009). The focus is on the development of the 'whole child' with an emphasis on the child's social role in the community.

In the UK, such ideas have influenced the development of thinking around community education, community work and youth work. Social and personal education, including health education, gained prominence during the 1970s and has continued in curriculum developments such as the introduction of personal, social and health education (PSHE) into the curriculum. One of the best-known examples of early experimentation with community approaches to education in the UK were the Cambridgeshire 'village colleges' of Henry Morris (1889–1961), closely linked to the necessity for community regeneration in rural areas. The aim was to bring together all the independent and potentially isolated activities of village life – the school, the library, adult learning, recreational classes, clubs, sport and village-hall activities – to create a new institution whilst preserving the unique identity of the constituent parts. Scotland has also had a long history of community education. The community schools initiative of 1999 perhaps comes closest to the community-based model of social pedagogy:

> Community learning and development is a way of listening and of working with people. We define this as informal learning and social development work with individuals and groups in their communities. The aim of this work is to strengthen communities by improving people's knowledge, skills and confidence, organisational ability and resources. Community learning and development makes an important contribution towards promoting lifelong learning, social inclusion and active citizenship.
>
> (Scottish Executive, 2003: para 1)

The involvement of youth work, community work and community-based adult learning is cited as being at the centre of dedicated expertise in this area. Other public-service disciplines such as health promotion, environmental protection, formal education and culture and leisure are also noted for adopting this approach.

A more traditional notion of education, especially in the UK, focuses on 'education-in-its-narrower-sense' (ENS). It 'equates education with schooling and certain kinds of formal learning focused wholly or mainly on cognitive capacities' (Moss and Haydon, 2008: 2). Here the focus narrows to that of ability, expected levels of achievement, targets and outcomes. Both concepts of education are concerned with learning, but education in its broadest sense (EBS) includes the social, aesthetic, ethical, cultural, emotional and physical domains as well as the purely cognitive and academic. This means that EBS can take place in a variety of settings and environments and involve a range of occupations and services as well as parents and teachers. Such learning is intentional and understood to be 'inextricably linked to care, health and other conditions needed to live a good life and for a democratic community to flourish: learning contributes to these conditions and these conditions enable learning' (ibid.: 3).

According to the Moss and Haydon analysis, this challenges the widespread assumption that education can only take place in schools. EBS 'decentres the school, teaching and the teachers in the discussion and practice of education' (ibid.: 3). It challenges understandings of the nature of school and the structures and practices which define it.

The extended schools agenda

It is the notion of the extended school that offers the greatest potential for a wider, more holistic approach to education. Community involvement (Chapter 8) and parental participation (Chapter 9) are promoted through *ECM*, most notably in extended schools. Schools can buy in or signpost a variety of services for children, young people and families, including family learning, parenting classes, sport and youth clubs and extra-curricular activities. Building on the *Sure Start* model the aim was to provide 'wrap-around care' for school-aged children. Public services such as health, social services and police could be co-located at school sites, creating what has been dubbed a system of 'Educare'. This has resonance with the vision of the Plowden Report (CACE, 1967) where services working together with a similar clientele could operate out of neighbourhood-based schools for greater effectiveness.

Since the nineteenth century, schools have offered health and welfare services to parents; however, the origins of full-service extended schools in the UK are first found in the US community schools movement of the 1930s. This gave adults as well as children in the local community access to school-based educational and recreational opportunities. More recently, American full-service schools have been promoted and researched by Joy Dryfoos (1994). Schools provide physical space for the operation of community services such as health and social care, making access to such services easier for family users. Full-service provision is about prevention, treatment and support and brings together state and local, public and private organisations. There is no single model of full-service extended schooling in the USA. Some

> involve the complete re-conceptualisation and re-organisation of the way in which health and education services are delivered. These approaches involve attempts to transform the school site into a central component of its community through the integrated and coordinated delivery of health, education and human services.
>
> (Wilkin *et al.*, 2003: i)

Whilst others reflect

> initiatives that extend the remit and programmes already existing within particular school environments by supplying additional services and facilities. School-based clinics and Family Service Centres act to support young people and their families in optimising their educational opportunities.
>
> (Wilkin *et al.*, 2003: i)

The aim of full-service extended schooling was to raise the educational attainment of those most likely to underachieve because of poverty and deprivation by dealing with attendant problems such as poor housing, health, nutrition, social welfare and family learning. The school becomes the hub of the community and service delivery: in other words a 'one-stop shop'. It is the *integration* rather than add-on nature of these services within the core business of the school that is significant in the US and community school models.

Whereas the US model seems to have emerged from a sense of dissatisfaction with the existing organisation of service delivery and subsequent fears for the most underprivileged, in the UK there was growing concern that schools alone could not tackle the complex issues of social exclusion and disadvantage (Wilkin *et al.*, 2003). The government's response was to promote the concept of multi-agency working (see Chapter 10). The introduction of Primary Care Trusts in the health services and Children's Trusts was to facilitate the move to more collaborative ways of working across health, education and social services in order to share the burden of responsibility. It seemed logical that schools could provide a base for the delivery of such multi-agency working, whilst at the same time reducing the burden on school staff through closer partnership with other services. The government White Paper *Schools Achieving Success* (DfES, 2001) suggested legislative changes that would enable schools to develop this approach. Pathfinder projects were funded in 2003 across twenty-five local authorities.

As in the case of the USA, there was no single interpretation of the full-service or extended school model in the UK. However, unlike the USA, the focus of English extended schools was on raising standards via the extension of existing educational or family support opportunities such as homework clubs, adult literacy, computer sessions and breakfast or after-school clubs. Rather than making schools the 'hub' of the community via the restructuring and delivery of a wide range of services, the government defined the extended school as 'one that provides a range of services and activities often beyond the school day to help meet the needs of its pupils, families and the wider community' (DfES, 2002: 5).

It is only a 'full-service' extended school that allows for the co-location of a range of services on the school premises. The core offer provided in or through extended mainstream and special schools was:

- high quality 'wrap-around' childcare provided on the school site or through other local providers, with supervised transfer arrangements where appropriate, available 8am–6pm all year round;
- a varied menu of activities to be on offer such as homework clubs and study support, sport (at least two hours a week beyond the school day for those who want it), music tuition, dance and drama, arts and crafts, special interest clubs such as chess and first aid courses, visits to museums and galleries, learning a foreign language, volunteering, business and enterprise activities;
- parenting support including information sessions for parents at key transition points, parenting programmes run with the support of other children's services and family learning sessions to allow children to learn with their parents;

- swift and easy referral to a wide range of specialist support services such as speech therapy, child and adolescent mental health services, family support services, intensive behaviour support, and (for young people) sexual health services. Some may be delivered on school sites;
- providing wider community access to ICT, sports and arts facilities, including adult learning.

(DfES, 2005a: 8)

All mainstream schools were expected to have such extended services in place by 2010. Cheminais (2007: 11) identifies four models for service delivery:

- direct delivery – schools (governing bodies) making arrangements themselves, employing staff, administering;
- delivery with third parties – working in partnership with exiting local, private or voluntary sector providers;
- linked with other schools in a cluster, Education Improvement Partner (EIP) or federation;
- co-locating with a children's centre.

These are underpinned by four philosophical approaches which focus and frame consultation with providers and users and the subsequent extended school provision:

- life skills (social capital) represented by voluntarism and trust; therapeutic activity and family learning;
- knowledge exchange (intellectual capital) focussing on exchanges of information, experimentation and enquiry; and training;
- multi-agency service centre (organisational capital) – adopting an holistic local approach, the co-location of services, SEN provision and inclusion;
- regeneration hub (human capital) – co-production, job and enterprise action, workplace learning.

(ibid.: 11)

The impact of the extended school agenda on teachers and classrooms was to vary from school to school depending on philosophical considerations and approaches to delivery. Those schools opting to signpost to services in the community or amongst a cluster of schools might experience very little change to their operational practices and core role; whereas those that adopted full-service models with the co-location of other agencies on-site would in effect be reconceptualising the very notion of 'school' and 'education'.

Teachers or pedagogues?

If *ECM* challenges the systems and structure of traditional schooling and its relationship with the wider community, it also challenges the role and professional identity of 'educationalists' both within the traditional schooling system and beyond, including youth and community work as well as those diverse agencies and occupations which collectively comprise the wider children's workforce. The European model of a social pedagogue may help to describe the new roles that were emerging for practitioners, including teachers, through engagement with the principles of *ECM*. Historically social work in Europe developed along two parallel modes of practice: the social caseworker who took a psychoanalytical approach, and the social pedagogue tradition which was underpinned by beliefs in social reform and 'renewing society through the skill of developing a person's inherent potential' (Higham, 2001: 24).

> The social pedagogue uses preventive, developmental, and educative forms of intervention with communities of users (not just children), and delivers ideas of developmental support through more informal means than classroom education. ... Social pedagogy promotes wellbeing through broadly based educational strategies. The social pedagogue prevents social problems by empowering people with knowledge and skills to manage their lives.
>
> (ibid.: 24)

There is an inextricable link between social/physical care roles and other aspects of upbringing, including formal education, which is similar to Bronfenbrenner's (1979) ecological view of human development (see Chapter 4). Moss and Haydon (2008) argue that all workers across the diverse settings mapped by EBS (and therefore *ECM*) could share a common identity as 'educators' or 'pedagogues', as well as maintaining specialist knowledge and competencies.

However, their analysis raises questions about:

- the type of curriculum suited to a broader understanding of education, especially if it is about lifelong development and learning;
- notions of inclusion/exclusion;

- the role of parents, especially in relation to the tensions between parents as clients and parents as strategic partners in the educational role of schools and other services;
- instrumentality and the outcomes focus of the current education system and *ECM*;
- the rights of the child.

Conclusion

Mechanisms such as multi-agency working, the adoption of lead professionals, the concept of a children's workforce defined by common skills and knowledge, an integrated qualifications framework and explicit outcomes for children and young people have all changed a once-familiar terrain. *ECM* revived the concept of holistic, child-centred education in the face of a dominant education discourse of targets, outcomes, competition and market forces. Again, this appeared to contradict the direction of government policies on teaching in the previous twenty years which had forced an agenda of target setting, assessment and accountability. *ECM* requires government and professions, including teachers, to re-examine the fundamental questions of whom we educate, why we educate, how we educate and where education takes place.

Chapter 12

Conclusion

Does every child matter?

Overview of *ECM* aims and principles

The key themes throughout this analysis of *Every Child Matters* have been the effects on society and policy-making of:

- capitalism and neo-liberalism;
- the modernisation of the welfare state with new public management;
- collaborative multi-agency working; and
- the political imperative of tackling social exclusion and deprivation.

New Labour's response in adopting the politics of the 'Third Way' created numerous, and to-date unresolved, tensions in the *ECM* agenda. Their aims were clear: to raise children and families out of poverty through a complex array of strategies that would tackle issues of healthcare, employment and education. Targeted support and initiatives were intended to make easier access to support services, while at the same time legislation enforced the principles of rights and responsibilities. Parents and children were redefined as stakeholders in the New Labour project, with expectations to benefit from and contribute to the five outcomes that it was believed would provide a more inclusive and cohesive society.

These aims and principles were reiterated in 2007 when Gordon Brown assumed the Labour premiership and created the Department for Children, Schools and Families (DCSF). The new plan was to build on the foundations of *ECM* in order to make England 'the best place in the world for children to grow up' (DCSF, 2007b: 3). Five underlying principles were made explicit:

- the government does not bring up children – parents do; so government needs to do more to back parents and families;
- all children have the potential to succeed and should go as far as their talents can take them;

- children and young people need to enjoy their childhood as well as grow up prepared for adult life;
- services need to be shaped by and responsive to children, young people and families, not designed around professional boundaries; and
- it is always better to prevent failure than tackle a crisis later.

(ibid.: 4)

The strategic objectives were listed as:

- Happy and healthy – securing the wellbeing and health of children and young people;
- Safe and sound – safeguarding the young and vulnerable;
- Excellence and equity – individual progress to achieve world-class standards and close the gap in educational achievement for disadvantaged children;
- Leadership and collaboration – system reform to achieve world-class standards and close the gap in educational achievement for disadvantaged children;
- Staying on – ensuring that young people are participating and achieving their potential to 18 and beyond;
- The right track – keeping children and young people on the path to success.

To this end the Children's Plan marked a continuation of the systematic and procedural reforms that characterised *ECM* with the heightened ambition of achieving 'world-class' status by 2020. Revised outcomes for *ECM* were published in 2008 (DCSF, 2008) making explicit, closer links with public service agreements (PSA) and the National Indicator Set (NIS) implemented in 2008. This continued the Labour government's commitment to modernising and monitoring local authority service delivery and their partnerships with other agencies. The NIS consisted of 198 national indicators for performance management of local government, 25 of which were to be determined by measuring citizen's views and perspectives. PSAs were first introduced through the 1998 Comprehensive Spending Review and focused on service delivery. Also revised in 2007 the new PSAs set out government priorities for the next two years and continued the philosophy of building services around citizens.

However, at the time of writing (November 2009) it seemed unlikely that New Labour would be in a position to continue these objectives into a new term of office. Trailing significantly in the opinion polls, it appeared improbable that they would win the next general election in May 2010. For political analysts and frontline workers alike the question was how far *ECM* would survive a new administration of a different political hue.

Indications from the major parties

New Labour and the *ECM* agenda must be credited with raising awareness of social exclusion and bringing the issues of family, community and safeguarding to the forefront of political debate. Indeed the policy initiatives that made up *ECM* had been accepted with little opposition from the key parties. Both the Liberal Democrats under Nick Clegg and the Conservatives under David Cameron made social justice and fairness central to their policy pronouncements in advance of the 2010 general election. Nick Clegg placed 'building a fairer society' second only to 'creating a sustainable economy' in his principles for government, *A Fresh Start for Britain* (Liberal Democrats, 2009). The Conservatives in their social reform policy sought a 'stronger, safer society, where opportunity is spread much more widely and fairly' (Conservative Party, 2009a: 4). Indeed Iain Duncan Smith, former leader of the Conservative Party, set up the independent think-tank, the Centre for Social Justice, in 2004 just two years prior to the demise of Labour's Social Exclusion Unit (SEU).

What distinguishes these political positions are different understandings of the role of the state and its relationship with local government and the governed. Nick Clegg called for a 'fairer dispersal and distribution of power' (Clegg, 2009: 11), laying claim to the 'progressive' role in British politics:

> A successful liberal democracy rests on the right balance between the legitimate powers of an accountable state and the freedoms of its citizens. As Mill said, 'a state which dwarfs its men ... even for beneficial purposes, will find that with small men no great things can be accomplished.'
>
> Underpinning this attitude towards power is a particular liberal attitude towards people – a belief that most people, most of the time, will make the right decisions for themselves, their family and their community. A belief in the dispersal of power only makes sense if sustained by this optimism.
>
> (ibid.: 6)

The Conservatives continued their traditional focus of wishing to 'roll back the state', diminish state intervention and protect and strengthen traditional (family) values. To this end the Conservatives pledged their support for *Sure Start* and children's centres and the philosophy of early intervention in the lives of families seemed set to continue (Conservative Party, 2009b). Greater powers and a reduction in bureaucracy were promised for local authorities in the attempt to turn back the tide of increased centralisaton under Labour. The interpretation of the role of the state and the relative out-workings of national and local government were to have serious implications for the *ECM* agenda.

The impact of the recession on government policy planning

Perhaps more significant in this discussion is the future role of the Treasury in funding such a complex agenda as *ECM*. It was the product of a high-spending Labour government which believed that state investment in the wellbeing of individual children and families would bring economic rewards: a highly trained workforce would allow Britain to compete in the global economy. State intervention was worth the financial cost for what it would finally bring. But *ECM* was not only the product of an interventionist Labour government which was prepared to invest national resources; it was the work of a Labour government which had access to high levels of state income. Education was only one of the areas in which Labour increased spending. Blair and Brown improved spending on the NHS and other social services; *ECM* was part of this government's growth in public expenditure. Labour did not raise taxes to fund these increases: it didn't need to. Since 1997 the gross domestic product (GDP) rose rapidly in a successful economy based on neo-liberal principles of unregulated markets, and state income rose in proportion, giving the government the opportunities it needed to invest. It is worth noting here that previous Labour governments during the 1960s and 1970s had planned for – even dreamed of – increased spending on schools and hospitals, but never had the resources to do it while the economy struggled. New Labour under Tony Blair, and its chancellor Gordon Brown, committed the party to the neo-liberal economic policies which generated economic wealth.

It is interesting to speculate as to how far a Conservative government would have sustained the funding for *ECM* with a strong and growing economy. And this would have been an ideological discussion: would Conservative policy which, as we have seen in earlier chapters, was to 'roll back government' and to diminish 'the nanny state', continue to invest in *ECM*? Blair and Brown had tiptoed between neo-liberal economics and state spending to create a marketised economy that would sustain high levels of public spending. Conservative thinking, on the other hand, is ideologically resistant to state intervention, for both economic and philosophical reasons. High public spending is seen as damaging to the economy, and intervention in the lives of families and individuals is anathema to the Conservative belief in individual liberty and independence.

From September 2008 the economic landscape changed dramatically and the confidence in neo-liberal free markets was rocked. Neo-liberal assumptions about global capitalism were challenged with the credit crunch and the crisis in international banking. Capitalism is based on investing to make profits. The desire to make more profits and bonuses led bankers and financial traders to take bigger and bigger risks in unregulated borrowing and lending. It all felt very good because there seemed to be lots of money. But on 9 September the American Lehman Brothers Bank collapsed because it had taken too many investment risks. There followed a run on all other banks and, on October 11, Dominique Strauss-Kahn, head of the International Monetary Fund (IMF) described the global economic financial system as 'close to meltdown': confidence in investment and profits was gone and a return to the economic slump of the 1930s threatened. The crisis left governments across the world struggling to prop up the financial system and attempting to restore confidence in the money markets by investing billions into their accounts. It was called 'recapitalisation', but could well be described as 'nationalisation'. It was the disaster predicted by the economist Joseph Stiglitz (2002, 2010) who had warned of the dangers of free-market capitalism in which governments are not permitted to intervene. In order for banks to keep up with the impetus and demands of the global economy, and without government intervention to curb excessive borrowing and lending, they were going to take more and more risks. Toynbee (2008: 25) describes the events as 'capitalism collapsing under the weight of its own self-contradictions'. She argued that market forces cannot be left to themselves: in the end, a strong state is needed to ensure economic stability.

The result of the credit crunch was economic recession across the world. Banks were unable to lend for investment and businesses were unable to flourish and to employ workers. Unemployment soared, interest rates collapsed and so did the income coming into governments from taxation. Gordon Brown in the UK convinced world leaders of the need for governments to intervene and to continue public spending in order to stimulate economic activity. To reduce public spending, he argued, would be to make the economy fall further behind. In addition, he argued for public investment in the economy through 'quantitative easing', the printing of more money to keep the economy moving. Most of the developed economies, including the United States, followed Britain's lead and maintained government spending. By the end of 2009, world economies were beginning to recover.

However, the means of government spending during this time of economic crisis when the government's income was reduced was state borrowing. Across the world governments had to borrow billions to maintain their economic policies, and Britain's debt was proportionally larger than all the others. It is at this point that the Labour Government and Conservative opposition came to blows. Conservatives had consistently argued for lower public spending; the policy of 'spending our way out of' the credit crunch had made government debt spiral. The national debt became the Conservatives' attack on Brown's government as irresponsible and spendthrift.

The political and economic future

With government debt running at £185bn at the end of 2009, the prospect for either party in government would be to reduce expenditure, and this was bound to threaten the future of *ECM*. However, there was a difference between the parties. Making national debt a political and an election issue, the Conservative Party was bound to commit itself to more dramatic cuts in public expenditure. At the Party's annual conference in October 2009, the shadow chancellor, George Osborne, explained that the Conservatives saw the solution to the economic crisis as reducing the national debt, which holds back the economy. Gordon Brown argued the opposite: that government spending is needed to support the economy.

While these opposing views are the stuff of economic theory, they have an immediate and direct effect on *ECM*: public spending in the scheme seemed to have more prospect under a Labour government than a Conservative one. However, the Conservative Party had in February 2009 committed itself to sustaining the *Sure Start* programme (Conservative Party, 2009a) This was interesting in that *Sure Start* seemed to have established itself as an essential social service which would be particularly difficult to dismantle. However, the expansion of *Sure Start* under Labour looked precarious. Iram Siraj-Blatchford, an adviser on early-years policy, commented to the DCSF Select Committee on 2 November 2009 that opening 3,500 children's centres would spread the funding too thinly and it would be better to have 500 which operated successfully (Ward, 2009).

While the economic future for *ECM* appeared bleak, during 2009 the political pressure to ensure the safeguarding of children increased. The media attention to the 'Baby P' case and similar events reinforced the need for well-organised state intervention which the Conservative Party was unable to resist.

Where are we heading?

In 2009 the centre-left think tank Demos set up the Progressive Conservative Project to explore 'how radical conservative philosophy, politics and policy can truly serve progressive goals'. Progressive Conservatism represents a break with the Thatcherite ideals of the 1980s and adopts a sceptical approach to the value of neo-liberal ideals of the free market. The Project was structured around four strands (Olliff-Cooper, 2009):

- democracy, community, neighbourhoods and power;
- family, childhood and society;
- markets, ownership, poverty, opportunity and wages;
- austerity, innovation, bureaucracy, and the shape of the state.

The latest report entitled *Leading from the Front* (Olliff-Cooper *et al.*, 2009) makes for interesting reading and focuses on public reform at a time of recession: how to 'make savings without making matters worse' (ibid.: 4). This involved sustainable cuts and empowering the frontline. Three principles are espoused:

- professionals should be liberated from bureaucracy and over management, freeing them to focus on serving the public;
- greater emphasis must be put on training and up-skilling in public services;
- accountability needs to be smarter and more effective – with greater freedom comes greater responsibility.

(ibid.: 4)

The argument is for empowering professionals to do the job they are trained for in order to empower citizens, and the report calls for several reforms:

- abolishing central auditing and replacing it with local control;
- up-skilling the front line;
- giving budget control to the front line;
- removing middle management;
- 'academising' all schools.

The report's deliberations on education focus on the devolution of greater power to schools and teachers. It picks up on New Labour's rhetoric of a 'world-class' education system and promotes this through the belief that the role of the state in education should be restricted to ensuring 'that professionals have suitable competency and training' (ibid.: 24). The recommendation is that the postgraduate certificate in education (PGCE) teacher-training course, currently one year, should be lengthened and include a higher entry requirement. Ongoing professional development would also be promoted with benefits for schools.

Overall, the Demos report shifts the focus of government attention on public services away from 'process' to 'performance'. Whatever the outlook for *ECM* in the new political climate, the children and families that inspired, in theory at least, one of the most radical changes to government policy since the 1988 Education Act must not be forgotten.

References

Adams, A. and Tucker, S. A. (2007) Every Child Matters: Change for children in schools, *Education 3–13*, 35 (3) 209–211.

Anderson, B (1983) *Imagined Communities: Reflections on the origin and spread of nationalism*. London: Verso.

Anderson, R., Brown, I., Clayton, R., Dowty, T., Korff, D. and Munro, E. (2006) *Children's Databases – Safety and Privacy: A report for the Information Commissioner.* Online. Available http://www.fipr.org/childrens_databases.pdf (accessed 10 October 2009).

Andrews, R. (2004) *Theorising the Third Way: Stakeholding, active citizenship and renewal*. Paper presented to RSA Conference 2004, Lincoln University.

Atkinson, M., Wilkin, A., Stott, A., Doherty, P. and Kinder, K. (2002) *Multi-agency Working: A detailed study.* Slough: NFER.

Ball, S. (2008) *The Education Debate.* Bristol: Policy Press.

Barnardo's Scotland (2007) *Index of Child Well-being in Scotland.* Edinburgh: Barnardo's. Online. Available www.barnardos.org.uk/wellbeing_for_children_in_scotland (accessed 27 September 2009).

Bell, L. and Stevenson, H. (2006) *Education Policy: Process, themes and impact.* Abingdon: Routledge.

Belsky, J. and Melhuish, E. (2007) Impact of Sure Start Local Programmes on Children and Families, in J. Belsky, J. Barnes and E. Melhuish (Eds.) (2007) *The National Evaluation of Sure Start: Does area-based early intervention work?* Bristol: Policy Press.

Beverton, S. (2001) Primary English Knowledge and Understanding, *Evaluation and Research in Education,* 15, (3) 128–135.

Blair, T. (1998) *The Third Way: New Politics tor the New Century*. London: Fabian Society.

Blair, T. (1999) http://news.bbc.co.uk/1/hi/uk_politics/298745.stm (accessed 20 October 2009).

Blewett, J. and Foley, P. (2008) Staying Safe, in J. Collins and P. Foley (Eds.) *Promoting Children's Wellbeing: Policy and practice.* Bristol: Policy Press.

Bradshaw, J., Hoelscher, P. and Richardson, D. (2007) An Index of Child Well-being in the European Union. *Social Indicators Research*, 80 (1) 133–177. Online. Available http://eprints.whiterose.ac.uk/1948/ (accessed 29 September 2009).

Bronfenbrenner, U. (1979) *The Ecology of Human Development: Experiments by nature and design*. Cambridge, MA: Harvard University Press.

Brown, P. and Lauder, H. (1997) Education, Globalisation and Economic Development, in A. H. Halsey, H. Lauder, P. Brown and A. Stuart Wells (Eds.) *Education: Culture, Economy and Class*. Oxford: Oxford University Press.

CACE (1967) *Children and their Primary Schools: A Report of the Central Advisory Council for Education* (The Plowden Report). London: Her Majesty's Stationery Office.

Callaghan, J. (1976) *Towards a National Debate*, Speech at a foundation stone-laying ceremony at Ruskin College, Oxford, October 18.

Centre for Economic and Social Inclusion and Child Poverty Action Group (2008) *Child Poverty Toolkit*. Online. Available http://www.childpovertytoolkit.org.uk/How-To-Use-The-Toolkit (accessed 3 July 2009).

Cheminais, R. (2007) *Extended Schools and Children's Centres: A practical guide*. Abingdon: Routledge.

Children Act (1989) www.opsi.gov.uk/Acts/acts1989/Ukpga_19890041_en_1.htm (accessed 9 November 2009).

Chitty, C. (2004) *Education Policy in Britain*. Basingstoke: Palgrave Macmillan.

Clarke, J. and Newman, J. (1997) *The Managerial State*. London: Sage.

Clarke, J., Hughes, G. and Lewis, G. (1998) Review, in G. Hughes and G. Lewis (Eds.) *Unsettling Welfare: The reconstruction of social policy*. London: RoutledgeFalmer.

Clegg, N. (2009) *The Liberal Moment*. London: Demos. Online. Available www.demos.co.uk (accessed 15 November 2009).

Communities and Local Government (2009) *Community Empowerment*. Online. Available http://www.communities.gov.uk/localgovernment/245624 (accessed 23 November 2009).

Conservative Party (2009a) *Repair: Plan for social reform*. London: Conservative Party. Online. Available www.conservatives.com/Policy/where_we_stand_/Family.aspx (accessed 15 November 2009).

Conservative Party (2009b) *Miller calls for improvements to Sure Start*. London: Conservative Party. Online. Available http://www.conservatives.com/News/News_stories/2009/02/Miller_calls_for_improvements_to_Sure_Start.aspx (accessed 7 November 2009).

Coombs, S. and Simon, C. A. (forthcoming) Designing accredited CPD for the Children's Workforce: Challenges and opportunities facing higher education in England. Submitted to *Journal of Professional Development in Education*.

Coulby, D. (2000) *Beyond the National Curriculum: School Knowledge and Society in UK and Europe*. London: RoutledgeFalmer.

Crozier, G. (2000) *Parents and Schools. Partners or Protagonists?* Stoke-on-Trent: Trentham Books.

CWDC (2007) *Multi-agency Working: Fact Sheet*. Online. Available http://www.dcsf.gov.uk/everychildmatters/resources-and-practice/IG00018 (accessed 12 November 2009).

CWDC (2009) *Progress Towards Integrated Working 2007–2008*. Leeds: CWDC. Online. Available www.cwdcouncil.org.uk/implementing-integrated-working/evaluating (accessed 12 November 2009).

Dale, R. and Robertson, S. (2008) *Reflections and Directions*, in K. Martens, A. Rusconi and K. Leutz (Eds.) *New Arenas of Global Governance and International Organisations*. London: Palgrave.

Daniels, H., Leadbetter, J. and Warmington, P. (2007) Learning in and for Multi-agency Working, *Oxford Review of Education*, 33 (4) 521–538.

Darling, A. (1997) A Political Perspective, in G. Kelly, D. Kelly and D. Gamble (Eds.) *Stakeholder Capitalism*. Basingstoke: Macmillan Press.

DCSF (2007a) *Every Child Matters: Change for Children ICS, CAF and ContactPoint – an Overview*. Online. Available http://www.dcsf.gov.uk/everychildmatters/strategy/deliveringservices1/caf/cafframework/ (accessed 9 November 2009).

DCSF (2007b) *The Children's Plan: Building Brighter Futures*. London: DCSF. Online. Available http://publications.dcsf.gov.uk/default.aspx?PageFunction=productdetails&PageMode=publications&ProductId=CM%207280 (accessed 15 November 2009).

DCSF (2008) *The Children's Plan: one year on*. London: DCSF. Online. Available http://www.dcsf.gov.uk/childrensplan/flagshipsummary/index.cfm?id=1821 (accessed 15 November 2009).

DCSF (2009a) *About Every Child Matters*. London: DCSF. Online. Available http://www.dcsf.gov.uk/everychildmatters/about/aims/childrenstrusts/childrenstrusts/ (accessed 20 October 2009).

DCSF (2009b) *Your Child, Your Schools, Our Future; building a 21st century schools system*. Norwich: The Stationery Office.

DCSF (2009c) *Improving the Educational Attainment of Children in Care*. London: DCSF. Online. Available www.teachernet.gov.uk/publications (accessed 9 November 2009).

DCSF (2009d) *Every Child Matters Outcomes Framework*. London: DCSF. Online. Available http://www.dcsf.gov.uk/everychildmatters/about/aims/outcomes/outcomescyp/ (accessed 15 November 2009).

Dean, H. (2003) *The Third Way and Social Welfare: The myth of post-emotionalism*. Online. Available http://eprints.lse.ac.uk/archive/00000354 (accessed 9 November 2009).

DfEE (1997) *Excellence for All Children: Meeting Special Educational Needs*. London: DfEE.

DfEE (1999) *Excellence in Cities*. London: DfEE.

DfEE and QAA (1998) *Education for Citizenship and the Teaching of Democracy in Schools*. London: DfEE. Online. Available http://www.qcda.gov.uk/libraryAssets/media/6123_crick_report_1998.pdf (accessed 11 November 2009).

DfES (2001) *Schools Achieving Success*. Nottingham: DfES Publications.

DfES (2002) *Extended Schools: Providing opportunities and services for all.* Nottingham: DfES Publications.

DfES (2003a) *Every Child Matters: Green Paper.* London: The Stationery Office.

DfES (2003b) *The Impact of Parental Involvement on Children's Education.* London: DfES. Online. Available http://publications.teachernet.gov.uk (accessed 11 November 2009).

DfES (2004a) *Every Child Matters.* London: DfES. Online. Available www.everychildmatters.gov.uk (accessed 4 July 2009).

DfES (2004b) *The Children Act.* London: TSO. Online. Available www.dfes.gov.uk (accessed 7 July 2009).

DfES (2004c) *Choice for Parents: The best start for children.* Nottingham: DfES Publications. Online. Available http://www.dcsf.gov.uk/everychildmatters/earlyyears/surestart/aboutsurestart/strategy/10yearstrategy/ (accessed 20 October 2009).

DfES (2004d) *Every Child Matters: Change for children in schools.* Nottingham: DfES. Online. Available www.everychildmatters.gov.uk (accessed 30 September 2009).

DfES (2005a) *Extended Schools: Access to services and opportunities for all.* Nottingham: DfES Publications.

DfES (2005b) *Common Core of Skills and Knowledge for the Children's Workforce.* Nottingham: DfES Publications. Online. Available http://www.everychildmatters.gov.uk/_files/37183E5C09CCE460A81C781CC70863F0.pdf (accessed 18 August 2008).

DfES (2006a) *Care Matters: Time for Change.* Norwich: TSO.

DfES (2006b) *Parenting Support: Guidance for Local Authorities in England.* Nottingham: DfES Publications. Online. Available www.everychildmatters.gov.uk (accessed 11 November 2009).

DfES (2006c) *Working Together to Safeguard Children.* Nottingham: DfES Publications. Online. Available www.everychildmatters.gov.uk/workingtogether/ (accessed 6 April 2008).

DfES (2006d) *Building a World-class Workforce for Children and Young People and their Families.* Nottingham: DfES Publications. Online. Available http://publications.teachernet.gov.uk (accessed 18 August 2008).

DfES (2006e) *Building an Integrated Qualifications Framework.* Nottingham: DfES Publications. Online. Available http://publications.teachernet.gov.uk (accessed 18 August 2008).

DfES (2007a) *Care Matters: Time for change.* Nottingham: DfES Publications.

DfES (2007b) *Every Parent Matters.* Nottingham: DfES Publications.

DH (1996) *Patient Partnership: Building a collaborative strategy.* London: Department of Health.

DH (2004) *National Service Framework for Children, Young People and Families.* London: DH Publications.

DirectGov (2009) *Parents' Rights and Responsibilities*. Online. Available http://www.direct.gov.uk/en/Parents/ParentsRights/DG_4002954 (accessed 25 November 2009).

Dryfoos, J. (1994) *Full-Service Schools: A revolution in health and social services for children, youth and families*. San Francisco: Jossey-Bass.

DWP (2009) *Households Below Average Income*. London: DWP. Online. Available http://research.dwp.gov.uk/asd/hbai.asp (accessed 2 November 2009).

Ellis, C. R. (2007) No Child Left Behind: A critical analysis: a nation at greater risk, *Curriculum and Teaching*, 9 (1&2), 221–233.

Evans, G. W., Eckenrode, J. and Marcynyszyn, L. (2007) *Poverty and Chaos*, First Unrie Bronfenbrenner Conference, Cornell University.

Family and Parenting Institute (2008) *Parenting Policy: The Last 10 Years* Online. Available http://www.familyandparenting.org/Filestore/Documents/Our_work/ParentingPolicyDevelopment.pdf

Fox Harding, L. (1997) *Perspectives in Child Care Policy*. London, Longman.

Frost, N. and Parton, N. (2009) *Understanding Children's Social Care; Politics, policy and practice*. London: Sage.

Gauvain, M. and Cole, M. (Eds.) (1993) *Readings on the Development of Children* (2nd Edn.) New York: Freeman.

Giddens, A. (2000) *The Third Way and its Critics*, Cambridge: Polity Press.

Glass, N. (1999) Sure Start: the development of an early intervention programme for young children in the United Kingdom, *Children and Society*, 13, 257–264.

Goldsmith (2008) *Citizenship: Our common bond*. Online. Available http://www.justice.gov.uk/reviews/docs/citizenship-report-full.pdf (accessed 11 November 2009).

Gray, R. and Francis, E. (2007) The Implications of US Experiences with Early Childhood Interventions for the UK SureStart Programme, *Childcare, Health and Development*, 33(6) 655–663.

Gyford, J. (1991) *Citizens, Consumers and Councils: Local Government and the public*. Houndmills: Macmillan.

Hannon, P., Pickstone, C., Sucking, R. and Crofts, D. (2008) The Reach of Early Intervention: A case study of a Sure Start programme, *Evidence and Policy* 4 (3) 205–225.

Harris, J. (1992) Political Thought and the Welfare State 1870–1940: A framework for British social policy, *Past and Present* 135 (May), 116–141.

Hayek, F. A. (1991) *The Road to Serfdom*, London: Routledge.

Heath, A. and Roberts, J. (2008) *British Identity: Its sources and possible implications for civic attitudes and behaviour*. Online. Available http://www.justice.gov.uk/reviews/docs/british-identity.pdf (accessed 3 October 2009).

Held, V. (2006) *The Ethics of Care: Personal, political and global*. Oxford: Oxford University Press.

Higham, P. (2001) Changing Practice and an Emerging Social Pedagogue Paradigm in England: The role of the personal advisor, *Social Work in Europe* 8 (1), 21–28.

HM Treasury (2002) *Spending Review: Opportunity and Security for All; Investing in an Enterprising, Fairer Britain*. London: HMSO. Online. Available http://www.hm-treasury.gov.uk/spend_sr02_repindex.htm (accessed 9 November 2009).

HM Treasury (2004a) *Child Poverty Review*. London: HMSO.

HM Treasury (2004b) *Spending Review: Stability, Security and Opportunity for All*. London: HMSO. Online. Available www.hm-treasury.gov.uk/spend_sr04_repindex.htm (accessed 9 November 2009).

HMSO (1921) *The Teaching of English in England (The Newbolt Report)*. London: HMSO.

HMSO (2003) *The Victoria Climbié Inquiry: Report of an Inquiry by Lord Laming*. London: HMSO. Online. Available www.victoria-climbie-inquiry.org.uk/finreport (accessed 9 September 2007).

HMSO (2004) *The Children Act*. Norwich: The Stationery Office.

Home Office (1968) *Report of the Inter-departmental Committee on Local Authority and Allied Personal Social Services. Joint memorandum*. London: HMSO. Online. Available http://filestore.nationalarchives.gov.uk/pdfs/small/cab-129–138-c-88.pdf (accessed 1 November 2009).

Hopkins, G. (2007) What have we learned? Child death scandals since 1944. *Community Care*, 11 January. Online. Available www.communitycare.co.uk (accessed 9 November 2009).

Hudson, B. and Hardy, B. (2002) What is 'successful' partnership and how can it be measured? in C. Glendinning, M. A. Powell and K. Rummery (Eds.) *Partnerships, New Labour and the Governance of Welfare*. Bristol: Policy Press.

Hutton, W. (1997) An Overview of Stakeholding, in G. Kelly, D. Kelly and D. Gamble (Eds.) *Stakeholder Capitalism*. Basingstoke: Macmillan Press.

IEA, International Association for the Evaluation of Educational Achievement (2007) *Brief History of IEA*. Amsterdam: IEA. Online. Available http://www.iea.nl/brief_history_of_iea.html (accessed 22 November 2009).

Isles, M. (2008) Children, families and the law in Collins, J. and Foley, P (Eds.) *Promoting Children's Wellbeing*. Bristol, Policy Press

James, O. (2007) *Affluenza*. London: Vermillion.

Joseph Rowntree Foundation (2009) *Child Poverty Programme: What can we do to end child poverty*? London: JRF. Online. Available www.jrf.org.uk/work/workarea/child-poverty (accessed 15 November 2009).

Kassem, D. (2006) Education of Looked-after Children: Who cares, in D. Kassem, E. Mufti and J. Robinson (Eds.) *Education Studies: Issues and critical perspectives*. Maidenhead: Open University.

Kettle, J. (2008) Children's Experience of Community Regeneration, in P. Jones, D. Moss, P. Tomlinson and S. Welch (Eds.) *Childhood: Services and Provision for Children*. London: Longman Pearson.

Laming (2009) *The Protection of Children in England: A progress report*. London: TSO.

Lauder, H. (1991) Democracy and Education, *British Journal of Sociology of Education*, 12 (4) 417–431.

Lee, D. and Newby H. (1983) *The Problem of Sociology: An introduction to the discipline*. London: Unwin Hyman.

Leverett, S. (2008) Parenting: politics and concepts for practice, in P. Foley and A. Rixon (Eds.) *Changing Children's Services: Working and learning together.* Bristol: Policy Press, in association with Milton Keynes: Open University Press.

Levitas, R. (2005) *The Inclusive Society?* Basingstoke: Palgrave Macmillan.

Liberal Democrats (2009) *A Fresh Start for Britain: choosing a different, better future*. London: Liberal Democrats. Online. Available http://freshstart.nickclegg.com/A Fresh Start for Britain.pdf (accessed 15 November 2009).

Lingard, B. and Ozga, J. (2007) Introduction, in B. Lingard and J. Ozga (Eds.) *The RoutledgeFalmer Reader in Education Policy and Politics*. Abingdon: Routledge.

Lupton, R. (2006) Schools in Disadvantaged Areas: Low attainment and a contextualised policy response, in H. Lauder, P. Brown, J. Dillabough and A. H. Halsey (Eds.) *Education, Globalisation and Social Change*. Oxford: Oxford University Press.

McNamara Horvat, E., Weinninger, E. B. and Lareau, A. (2006) From Social Ties to Social Capital: Class differences in the relations between schools and parent networks, in H. Lauder, P. Brown, J. Dillabough and A. H. Halsey (Eds.) *Education, Globalisation and Social Change*. Oxford: Oxford University Press.

Moon, M. J. (2002) The Evolution of e-government among the Municipalities: rhetoric or reality, *Public Administration Review*, 62 (4) 424–433.

Moore, R. (2004) *Education and Society: Issues and Explanations in the Sociology of Education*, Cambridge, Polity Press.

Moss, P. (2004) Sure Start, *Journal of Education Policy,* 19 (5) 631–634.

Moss, P. and Haydon, G. (2008) *Every Child Matters and the Concept of Education,* London: Institute of Education, University of London,

NCEE, National Commission on Excellence in Education (1983) *A Nation at Risk: The imperative for educational reform*. Washington DC: NCEE. Online. Available http://www.ed.gov/pubs/NatAtRisk/risk.html (accessed 10 October 2009).

NESS (National Evaluation of Sure Start) Research Team (2005) *Implementing Sure Start Local Programmes: An Integrated Overview of the First Four Years.* London: HMSO

NFER (2006) *Analysis of CYPPs 2006*. Nottingham: NFER. Online. Available www.nfer.ac.uk/emie (accessed 3 July 2009).

ODPM (2004) *The Egan Review: Skills for sustainable communities*. London: ODPM.

OECD (1996) *Measuring What People Know: Human capital accounting for the knowledge economy*. Paris: OECD.

Olliff-Cooper, J. (2009) *Resuscitating Democracy.* London: Demos. Online. Available www.demos.co.uk (accessed 15 November 2009).

Olliff-Cooper, J., Wind-Cowie, M. and Bartlett, J. (2009) *Leading from the Front.* London: Demos. .

Olssen, M., Codd, J. and O'Neill, A. (2004) *Education Policy: Globalisation, citizenship and democracy.* London: Sage.

Orfield, G. (2004) Introduction, in G. L. Sundermann and J. Kim (Eds.) *Inspiring Vision, Disappointing Results: Four studies on implementing the No Child Left Behind Act.* Cambridge, MA: Civil Rights Project, Harvard University.

Parenting Academy (2007) *Launch of National Academy for Parenting Practitioners today signals a step change in driving up the quality of parent services.* Press Release 21, Nov.

Parker, S. and Gallagher, N. (2007) *The Collaborative State: How working together can transform public services.* London: Demos.

Paton, G. (2009) OECD: UK has more 'Neets'. *The Daily Telegraph,* 8 September.

Power, S., Whitty, G., Gerwitz, S., Halpin, D. and Dickson, M. (2004): Paving a 'third way?' A policy trajectory analysis of education action zones, *Research Papers in Education,* 19 (4) 453–473.

Putnam, R. (1995) Bowling Alone: America's Declining Social Capital, *Journal of Democracy,* 6 (1) 65–78.

Putnam, R. D. (1993) The Prosperous Community: Social capital and public life, *The American Prospect*, 4: 13. Online. Available http://www.prospect.org/cs/archive (accessed 11 November 2009).

Rand, A. (1964) *The Virtue of Selfishness.* New York: Signet.

Rudalevige, A. (2003) The Politics of No Child Left Behind, *Education Next,* 3 (4) 62–69.

Rustin M. (2004) Learning from the Victoria Climbié Inquiry, *Journal of Social Work Practice,* 18 (1) 9–18.

Rutter, M. (2007) Sure Start Local Programmes: An outsider's perspective, in J. Belsky, J. Barnes and E. Melhuish (Eds.) *The National Evaluation of Sure Start: Does area-based early intervention work?* Bristol: Policy Press.

Scottish Executive (2003) *Working and learning together to build stronger communities. Working draft Community Learning and Development Guidance, Edinburgh.* Edinburgh: Scottish Executive. Online. Available http://www.infed.org/archives/gov_uk/working_together.htm (accessed 12 November 2009).

SEU (1998) *Bringing Britain Together: A national strategy for neighbourhood renewal.* London: The Stationery Office

SEU (2005) *Making it Happen in Neighbourhoods: The National Strategy for Neighbourhood Renewal.* London: SEU. Online. Available http://www.communities.gov.uk/communities/neighbourhoodrenewal/?did=1193 (accessed 11 November 2009).

Sharland, E., Taylor, I., Jones, L., Orr, D. and Whiting, R. (2007) *Inter-professional Education for Qualifying Social Work.* London: Social Care Institute for Excellence.

Smith, M. K. (2001) *'Community' in the Encyclopedia of Informal Education,* Online. Available http://www.infed.org/community/community.htm (accessed 11 November 2009).

Smith, M. K. (2004, 2005) Extended schooling – some issues for informal and community education, *The Encyclopaedia of Informal Education*. Online. Available www.infed.org/schooling/extended_schooling.htm (accessed 12 November 2009).

Smith, M. K. (2009) Social pedagogy, *The Encyclopaedia of Informal Education*. Online. Available http://www.infed.org/biblio/b-socped.htm (accessed 12 November 2009).

Smith, N. and Middleton, S. (2007) *Poverty Dynamics Research in the UK*, York: Joseph Rowntree Foundation.

Social Trends 32, *Voting Turnout by Age and Gender*. London: Office for National Statistics. Online. Available http://www.statistics.gov.uk/STATBASE/ssdataset.asp?vlnk=5204&More=Y (accessed 3 October 2009).

Statistical First Release (2009) *Children Looked After in England (including adoption and care leavers) year ending 31 March 2009*. London: DCFS. Online. Available www.dcsf.gov.uk/rsgateway/DB/SFR/ (accessed 3 September 2009).

Stiglitz, J. (2002) *Globalization and its Discontents*. London: Penguin.

Stiglitz, J. (2010) *Freefall: Free markets and the sinking of the global economy*. London: Allen Lane.

Sylva, K., Meluish, E., Sammons, P., Siraj-Blatchford, I. and Taggart, B. (2004) *The Effective Provision of Pre-School Education (EPPE) Project, Technical paper 12, Final Report*, London: DfES/Institute of Education, University of London.

Taylor, S., Rizvi, F., Lingard, B. and Henry, M. (1997) *Educational Policy and the Politics of Change*. London: RoutledgeFalmer.

Teisman, G. R. and Klijn, E.-H. (2002) Partnership Arrangements: Governmental rhetoric or governance scheme, *Public Administration Review*, 62 (2), 189–198.

Thomas, G. and Hocking, G. (2003) *Other People's Children: Why their quality of life is our concern*. London: Demos.

Thrupp, M. and Hursh, D. (2006) The limits of managerialist school reform: The case of target-setting in England and the USA, in H. Lauder, P. Brown, J.-A. Dilabough and A. H. Halsey (Eds.) *Education, Globalization and Social Change* Oxford: Oxford University Press.

Tolofari, S. (2005) New Public Management and Education, *Policy Futures in Education*, 3(1) 75–98.

Tomlinson, S. (2005) *Education in a Post-welfare Society*. Maidenhead: Open University Press.

Townsend, I. and Kennedy, S. (2004) *Poverty: Measures and Targets*. House of Commons Research Paper 04/23.

Townsend, P. (1979) *Poverty in the United Kingdom*. London: Penguin Books and Allen Lane.

Toynbee, P. (2008) Wanted: a leader who dares draw some bright red lines. *The Guardian*, 20 September, p. 25.

Trudge, J. (2008) *Everyday Lives of Young Children: Culture, class and childrearing in diverse societies*. Cambridge: Cambridge University Press.

UNCHR (United Nations Commission for Human Rights) (1989) *Convention on the Rights of the Child.* Online. Available http://www2.ohchr.org/english/law/crc.htm (accessed 2 September 2009).

UNICEF Innocenti Research Centre (2007) Report Card 7: *Child Poverty in Perspective: an overview of child well-being in rich countries.* Florence: UNICEF Innocenti Research Centre. Online. Available http://www.unicef.org/media/files/ChildPovertyReport.pdf (accessed 3 October 2009).

US Department of Education (1991) *America 2000: An Education Strategy.* Washington DC: Sourcebook.

US Department of Education (1994) *Goals 2000: Educate America Act.* Online. Available www.ed.gov/legislation/GOALS2000/TheAct/ (accessed 31 October 2009).

US Department of Education (2001) *No Child Left Behind: The Elementary and Secondary School Act 2001.* Online. Available www.ed.gov/legislation/ESEA02/ (accessed 4 April 2009).

Vincent, C. (1996) *Parents and Teachers: Power and participation.* Lewes: Falmer Press.

Vleminckx, K. and Smeeding, T. (2001) *Child Well-being, Child Poverty and Child Policy in Modern Nations: What do we know?* Bristol: Polity Press.

Walker, G. (2008a) Safeguarding Children: Visions and values, in P. Jones, D. Moss, P. Tomlinson and S. Welch (Eds.) *Childhood, Services and Provision for Children.* Harlow: Pearson Education.

Walker, G. (2008b) *Working Together for Children: A critical introduction to multi-agency working.* London: Continuum.

Ward, H. (2009) Sure Start for all will be a damp squib. *Times Educational Supplement,* 6 November, p. 6.

Ward, S. (2008) Education Policy and Politics, in S. Ward (Ed.). *A Student's Guide to Education Studies.* Abingdon: Routledge.

Ward, S. and Eden, C. (2009) *Key issues in Education Policy.* London: Sage.

Welch, S. (2008) Childhood: Rights and realities, in P. Jones, D. Moss, P. Tomlinson and S. Welch (Eds.) *Childhood: Services and Provision for Children.* Harlow: Pearson Longman.

Wilkin, A., Kinder, K., Whire, R., Atkinson, M. and Doughty, P. (2003) *Towards the Development of Extended Schools.* Slough: NFER.

Wilkinson, R. and Pickett, K. (2009) *The Spirit Level: Why more equal societies almost always do better.* London: Allen Lane.

Wind-Cowie, M and Olliff- Cooper, J. with Bartlett, M. (2009) *Leading from the Front.* London: Demos.

Woman's Own (1987) Douglas Keay interview with Margaret Thatcher, 31 October, pp. 8–10.

Woodhall, M. (1997) Human Capital Concepts, in A. H. Halsey, H. Lauder, P. Brown and A. S. Wells (Eds.) *Education: Culture, Economy, Society.* Oxford: Oxford University Press.

Woodward, L. (1985) *The Oxford History of England: The Age of Reform 1815–1870.* Oxford: Clarendon Press.

Index